Shut Up and Manage

A Quiet Leader's Guide to Engaging Others

◇———◆◆———◇

M.J. Clark

Shut Up and Manage: A Quiet Leader's Guide to Engaging Others makes a great gift, teaching tool, and/or self-help guide. For more information (including information on bulk purchases for friends, family, employees, or members of your group or organization), contact the author at mj@mjclarkbooks.com.

This book is presented for informational and educational purposes only. The material contained herein is sold and/or otherwise made available with the understanding that the publisher and/or author are not giving career, legal, or any other type of professional or personal advice of any kind. The contents of this book are derived from the author's personal experience, but neither implies nor intends any guarantee of accuracy or effectiveness. The author and publisher believe the information to be sound but cannot be held responsible for actions taken by readers nor the results of those actions. Readers should seek competent professional advice before making any decisions. The author and publisher shall have no liability or responsibility to any person or entity with respect to any loss or damages caused, or alleged to be caused, directly or indirectly by the information in this book.

Editing by Hannah Magnusson, Great Grey Editorial,
https://www.greatgreyeditorial.com
Cover art by 100 Covers, https://100covers.com/

Bonus: Free Gift!

As a way of saying thanks for your purchase, I'm offering a free digital product for busy managers that is exclusive to readers of *Shut Up and Manage*:

Intentional Living Guide:

Four Tips and a Template for Making the Most of Your Time

Do you often feel guilty because you just spent several hours watching TV or scrolling through social media when you could have done something more productive with some of that time? Use this guide to calculate how you are currently spending your time and decide how to reallocate your available hours.

Get your guide by visiting: https://bit.ly/3axRMI8.

Foreword

By Tammy S. (O'Neill) Grimes

C uriously enough, about the time I met M.J. Clark, I was beginning my first managerial role at American Red Cross as the Director of Communications in the mid-1990s. Fresh off nearly five years of managing PR and publications at St. Ann's Hospital and "managing" non-paid volunteers all those years, as well as counseling students who were part of the Public Relations Student Society of America program at five Ohio universities, I felt ready for prime time and a formal managing role.

Little did I know all that I needed to learn. As the youngest child of six growing up in northeast Ohio, I felt a need to speak out and be noticed and heard, as no one else would do it for me. As a self-proclaimed extrovert, I felt proud and ready to step into the shoes of a retiring director more than twice my age, feeling I had something to prove. I quickly learned that formal management required me to be a little quieter, to listen more, to delegate, and to motivate and reward in new ways (beyond the money and budget afforded me). I learned the importance of being behind the scenes, when to encourage, and how to get more mileage and engagement from volunteers and formal reports alike.

I was cutting my teeth and thankfully had patient leaders and peers who helped me do that. I learned from them what it meant to engage and trust for the greatest results. There I had the accountability for guiding communications across multiple counties throughout central Ohio to ensure a viable blood supply, and I had the privilege of working with hundreds of volunteers again - at the board level, community partnerships with PR agencies, local media and even the International Association of Fire Fighters and the Federal Order of Police.

Who knew getting folks to donate their time and blood would have been my learning ground for managing and engaging others, just a few under my formal management structure, and hundreds more to be influenced? There I learned the power of leadership, collaboration and the engagement needed to advance business results one person at a time. Another wise female leader who challenged the perfectionist in me there taught me the power of stopping the hamster wheel of ideas waking me at night and keeping a notebook by my nightstand, much like M.J. advises in her chapter on organization.

Luckily, M.J. happened to be one of the amazing students at Ohio University I met and had the opportunity to encourage and guide. Now, I'm proud to say she's not only one of my greatest teachers, but I call her a life-long friend and colleague. M.J. is a leader who puts her authentic and transparent self forward always - whether as a friend, wife, mother, sibling or consultant. She is a learner for life who continues to research and learn, taking her research and combining it with life experience, to give practical advice and nuggets of wisdom to counsel and coach others.

Since my days at American Red Cross, I've had the honor of working for great health systems and corporations between Ohio and Arizona, spending nearly two decades of my life most recently with many brilliant minds and managers at Intel Corporation. While I've had only one formal management role in those years, being a senior individual contributor in a global organization with more than 100,000 employees has taught me the value of managing from the seat that I am in - whether that's as a team lead or member.

Being part of teams rolling out benefits and services to all our employees or leading business group communications around the world for divisions as small as 1,300 or as big as 40,000, I've learned the power of being part of a team - all the aspects that M.J. covers in her chapters can apply to those in formal manager roles and even to those who aren't. Sometimes I get to lead and influence, and sometimes I follow, but the power of we and teams are so much greater than me or I.

In closing, I'll share a recent opportunity I had in Phoenix when M.J. came to speak at an engagement with the American Academy of College Nurses in April 2019. I took vacation to witness her in action and play assistant for the day. Seeing the lightbulbs go off and the excitement and passionate engagement from the attendees gave me even more appreciation for my friend. Her magnetism was catching and effective, giving these professionals who already had decades of experience new skill sets to add to their toolbox to try out. Give this book a read. No matter what level you are in an organization - new or seasoned, management or not - you will walk away with salient points to use in your professional and personal lives. And remember on your journey, progress over perfection!

- Tammy S. (O'Neill) Grimes, BSJ
  (Ohio University 1987)

Dedication

To my amazing clients, both past and present. Thank you for helping me continue to learn best practices in management by allowing me a front row seat to your challenges, thoughts, emotions, and decision-making. I consider it a great honor to be trusted with your truth.

CONTENTS

Introduction

---

hy would anyone *want* the job of managing, coaching or mentoring other people? These activities take time and energy away from our own work. Often, the people we attempt to help in these ways are reluctant participants and are not even appreciative of our efforts!

Some are reluctant leaders - people thrown into leadership or management roles who don't want to be there, but also don't want to fail.[1] Why is this? Why do we care? Why do we even accept management and leadership roles?

I believe our purpose on this earth is, put simply, to connect. Professor Peter Cohen, Director of the Centre for Drug Research in Amsterdam, agrees, saying that "human beings have a deep need to bond and form connections. It's how we get our satisfaction. If we can't connect with each other, we will connect with anything we can find," including drugs, alcohol, gambling, and cheesecake. Many people think the opposite of addiction is sobriety. But Cohen argues the opposite of addiction is human connection.[2]

If we are hard-wired for connection, it makes sense that we want to form bonds with others in our personal and work lives, even if it's difficult at times.

I wrote my first book, *Shut Up and Lead: A Communicator's Guide to Quiet Leadership*, because in my quest to form bonds with others, I talked way too much. I found that listening more attentively and curbing my natural desire as an extrovert to process information out loud fostered more connection. My first book explores how leaders can become more powerful by being more intentional in their communication and fostering better listening skills. I'm writing this book, *Shut Up and Manage*, for all the quiet leaders who want to more effectively manage and engage others.

In my many years of executive coaching with CEOs and blue-collar workers alike in a variety of fields, I have found many managers face the same challenges. I wrote this book to answer the questions I continue to receive from clients who simply seek to connect. I will use that inside knowledge of those common challenges they've shared with me to help you:

- Communicate more effectively

- Develop trust with others

- Become more organized

- Hire, onboard, train and motivate direct reports

- Keep people accountable

- Achieve goals

Section One: Start With Self begins with a review of basic management principles. In Chapter One, I'll outline the differences between leadership and management, and how we can adapt to those who possess the skills that elude us. Chapter Two is filled with ideas for getting more organized in order to become more consistent and productive. When we show consistency, we gain the trust of our colleagues. Chapter Three will offer tips about how to plan properly to achieve goals. I will also offer ideas for self-accountability.

Section Two: Encourage Excellence begins with Chapter Four, where I will offer ideas for hiring and onboarding new employees, as well as ways to effectively praise new employees to create early engagement. In Chapter Five, I will describe how to create healthy relationships with others at work, without overstepping bounds that make keeping others accountable difficult.

In Chapter Six, I will explore more advanced concepts of communication that will help readers effectively lead and manage others. These concepts include Actor-Observer Bias, adjusting our preferences to better understand and relate to others, how to foster empathy with those who are different from us, and recognizing cultural differences.

Chapter Seven outlines how to effectively keep your direct reports and peers accountable. We'll also discuss the different levels of workload various employees can handle. Chapter Eight gives tips on how to develop trust and explores the notion of starting with trust instead of expecting others to earn our trust. In this chapter, we'll also talk about setting boundaries to keep others from taking advantage of us. In Chapter Nine, how to motivate others and delegate appropriately will be explored. The chapter offers low-cost ideas for motivating team members as well as strategies to delegate effectively.

The Third Section: Review and Restructure, allows us to explore how to properly evaluate and terminate, when necessary, our staff members. Chapter Ten offers techniques for empowering those who report to you. Chapter Eleven offers advice on how to utilize formal and informal reviews to evaluate employees in a way that motivates them to strive for excellence. Chapter Twelve reviews the part of our job most managers dread: firing others. Although each organization has a unique process for how they terminate employees, we'll explore some best practices, including some to keep your organization from being sued.

In striving to become an effective manager, I've learned the hard way: from my mistakes. And I've made a lot! Unfortunately, we are never done making mistakes, so I continue to be a work in progress.

After working in corporate, non-profit, state and federal government, and professional services settings, as well as running my own consulting business for more than a decade, I want to share what I've learned. I have read many management books throughout the years, and I find what's missing are suggestions for practical application of the principles taught. My hope is that this book's real-life examples and suggestions for implementation will empower managers to try new ways of fine-tuning management skills and connecting with others that will lead to employee engagement and trust building.

In addition, I've asked some of the most effective managers I know to offer my readers tips based on what they know now that they wish they knew earlier in their career. These Pro Tips will appear at the end of each chapter.

After reading this book, you will be able to practice specific techniques that will help you improve your management skills over time. This is not a light switch, but a process. Patience, practice, and courage are all you need to succeed.

You may feel like this will not work for you, but I assure you that if you can believe it, you can achieve it. I went from a passive doormat to an assertive, confident executive, and I will explain in Chapter Six how changing my thinking started me on this life-altering path.

For now, let's begin by focusing on the roles of leaders and managers and how we can adjust to the different preferences of the people typically in those roles.

Section One: Start with Self

"The first key to leadership is self-control."

- Jack Weatherford

Basic Management Principles

L eadership and management are two very different functions, even though they overlap in many roles. Both are important to running a successful business. Most leaders, like managers, have direct reports they supervise, so they are leading and managing at different times throughout their day or week.

Leadership and management are both nouns (positional) and adjectives (describing a skill). Having a leadership title doesn't mean you show leadership ability in your actions, just as being given a management position doesn't mean you have exceptional management skills.[3]

Organizational Leadership is "the ability of an individual to influence, motivate, and enable others to contribute toward the effectiveness and success of the organizations of which they are members."[4] Most effective leaders are imaginative, big-picture, visionary, systems thinkers. They are typically willing to take calculated risks. One can have a leadership title and still not be perceived as a leader if he doesn't possess leadership attributes.

In addition, those who demonstrate leadership characteristics can lead from any position in a company. A team leader, if we disregard positional titles, is generally someone who greatly surpasses other team members in his or her ability to influence the group.[5] While a leader might envision and share where she sees the company in ten years, a manager will direct staff day-to-day to fulfill that vision.

Management is directing and controlling one or more people to accomplish goals. Most effective managers are rational, organized, detail-oriented, creative problem solvers and master delegators. Management, to me, is like raising kids. If you are a parent or caregiver, you know the challenge in trying to cajole a reluctant child to do his homework, help around the house, or be nice to his sibling. In the workplace, managers often have to cajole reluctant direct reports to do their work, collaborate with team members, and get along with co-workers. In fact, we can apply many of the principles discussed in this book to parenting.

I will never forget a conversation I had with my current supervisor, the president of Integrated Leadership Systems, many years ago. He was explaining in very broad strokes a new service he wanted me to offer to clients. As I listened, I struggled to come up with a way to implement (or even just communicate to clients) what he was suggesting. I asked a couple of very specific questions to help me wrap my brain around this concept he was sharing, and he looked at me and said, "M.J., you're missing the whole point." I responded,

"I think you are missing the point. I can't sell or deliver what I don't understand."

I didn't know it at the time, but we were both missing the point. The point is to fully understand each other. He was presenting something to me in a visionary way, and I was trying to operationalize it. We weren't thinking about it in the same way at all, and it frustrated both of us that the other "didn't get it."

Over my career, I have continually sought new ways to adapt my communication style to suit other managers and leaders, some of whom are very visionary, big-picture thinkers and others who are more process-focused, detail-oriented executives. When engaging a visionary leader who thinks more globally, it works well for me to speak concisely and refrain from asking process-related questions. These leaders typically don't want the details to get in the way of achieving the goal. They tend to have a "get it done" mentality and leave it to others to figure out how. This is wonderful for direct reports who prefer autonomy and are excited by the challenge of solving problems and creating new processes and procedures.

When dealing with someone who is more process-oriented, it's effective to talk through a loose outline of how the idea you're presenting might be implemented. For me, it helps to have a kernel of an idea about the implementation, even though it will evolve as I think about it more thoroughly later. It gives me comfort to have a concept and starting point. If you are a visionary person about to present a big idea to a structured thinker, try to come up with a loose outline of how it might be implemented or, at least, anticipate questions about implementation.

Accountability is an important part of this mix and will be addressed thoroughly in Chapter Seven. For now, let's agree that as managers, we must coach and provide constructive feedback to help subordinates grow and thrive. It's important to acknowledge people's strengths and offer them opportunities to shine.

It's also helpful to approach direct reports with honesty and the courage to have tough conversations when they are not meeting expectations. They can't grow if they don't know how they can improve. A productive approach is to recognize their leadership (visionary) or management (detailed) preference and pair that with their strengths to assign them work that will be of interest. It's much easier to keep people accountable when they love what they do.

Developing effective, healthy teams is a challenge common to both managers and leaders. What appear to be great, individual team members on paper don't always translate to such when team dynamics and politics are at play. You can have a football team filled with great individual contributors, but if they can't trust one another and focus on the team's success, they will undoubtedly lose games.

How do you confront an otherwise productive employee who engages in passive aggressive behavior? What can you do to motivate someone to stop procrastinating? Can you change unhealthy competitive behavior on a team to interdependent behavior where everyone wins? We will explore these and other questions about how to create great teams and communicate more effectively in Chapters Five, Six and Seven.

It's easy to point at all the imperfections of those we manage. Looking in the mirror is much tougher. For now, let's consider how we can become better at managing ourselves. As a supervisor, are you working on improving your emotional intelligence, so you can be composed under pressure? In my experience as an executive coach, I've learned this is one area in which most people (including me!) could improve.

Emotional intelligence is the ability to identify, understand and manage our emotions. Self-awareness is the cornerstone of emotional intelligence. At ILS, we recommend journaling to all our clients. Searching for deeper meaning by spending time writing about how we think and feel helps us develop emotional intelligence. We can't control our emotions unless we can identify them and understand when negative emotions are likely to surface. Journaling, over time, enables us to identify patterns in our thoughts that lead to negative emotions and, ultimately, unhelpful behavior. We better understand situations that trigger negative emotions when we take time to journal.

In addition to journaling, I'll share one more thing I learned to do on my own that may be of help in this area. I was having an awful day, and I was in the car with my husband and two pre-teen sons driving to Florida for a vacation, and I was complaining and crabby and being snippy with everyone. I was in a terribly grumpy mood. I stopped for a minute, and then I said out loud, "I can't even stand myself right now. How can all of you even stand to be in this car with me when I'm behaving so ridiculously?"

My question was met with stunned silence. I then said, "I wish human beings had a refresh button like we do on the internet. Then I could just push that button and take away my crummy attitude. I want to have a great vacation, and this isn't helping us start out on a positive note. I paused to think some more. "You know what?" I asked rhetorically. "I'm going to mentally press the refresh button and begin again. I'm pressing it right now."

I heard a couple of giggles from the kids in the back seat. I began again, intentionally choosing my mood instead of just allowing events of the day to dictate it for me. I began by asking the kids how their day was and talking with my husband about our trip in a pleasant tone. After that day, if one of us was being grouchy and suffering from a bad attitude, another family member would say to them, "You need to press the refresh button."

Over a decade later, I'm still using this mental technique to self-regulate my moods. It requires objective consideration of how I want to show up in each situation, without simply succumbing to external factors. People don't "make" us mad and negative circumstances don't "ruin our whole weekend." *We* do these things, based on our poor reactions to people and circumstances. We can absolutely choose our emotional states.

Chapter Six describes how you can use the principles of cognitive behavior therapy to better understand and change the way you think in order to control your emotions. Understanding and applying that concept is the very essence of practicing emotional intelligence.

Pro Tip from Owen Wyss, Chief Financial Officer at Thompson Concrete

Stop focusing on your response and listen! Too often I find myself catching just the first few words of a conversation and then drifting off into my own head to begin crafting my response. If only I knew the things I've missed and opportunities I've wasted because I thought I needed ample time to develop a well-reasoned response - but for what? So I could win the conversation, prove how smart I am, get the conversation over as quickly as possible?

I'm sure each conversation differed, but for me, it was mostly a desire to prove how worthy and/or smart I am. All that did, though, was make me miss key details of the conversation and non-spoken social, verbal and physical cues, together accounting for prime missed opportunities to demonstrate my true abilities to lead through my thorough understanding of the problem and, more importantly, the person I was conversing with.

Instead of crafting my response, I should have been focused on listening, to pick up on the needs of the person on the other end - their needs in the moment, their needs as a person and their needs as a leader. Your audience will convey more about their needs than just what is said verbally, if you as a leader are willing to open up, listen, see and feel all of the available cues.

If I could have just spent more time listening, and in turn more time understanding the needs of those around me, as a leader, I could have provided that validation for them while at the same time leading in the direction I thought best. As a result, I would have been developing into a thorough and thoughtful leader who had other than just the best interests of himself in mind. Instead, though, I focused on me and my needs, and that held me back, and still continues to do so to this day.

Your audience will give you time to work on your response, and, in fact, will likely respect it more if you spend time listening to them in full and understanding both their immediate and long-term goals and needs. Seeing all of their needs and responding accordingly (also a tough skill to develop, as it requires an accurate understanding of the person/group and pairing of a response) will build the following you are looking for.

Chapter One – Key Points

- Leadership is the ability of an individual to influence, motivate, and enable others to contribute to the overall success of the organization.

- Management is directing and controlling one or more people to accomplish goals.

- When communicating with visionary, big-picture thinkers, it can be helpful to talk concisely and refrain from asking process-related questions.

- When communicating with someone who is process-oriented, it's effective to talk through a loose outline of how the idea you're presenting might be implemented.

- As managers, we must coach and provide constructive feedback to help subordinates grow and thrive:

- Acknowledge people's strengths.

- Offer them opportunities to shine.

- Approach direct reports with honesty and the courage to have tough conversations when they are not meeting expectations.

- Recognize their leadership (visionary) or management (detailed) preference and pair that with their strengths to assign them work that will be of interest.

- Emotional intelligence is the ability to identify, understand and manage our emotions, and self-awareness is the cornerstone of emotional intelligence.

- Journaling enables us to identify patterns in our thoughts that lead to negative emotions and, ultimately, unhelpful behavior. It also helps us understand situations that trigger our negative emotions.

- When you realize your bad mood is negatively impacting yourself and/or those around you, mentally press the "refresh" button and begin again on a more positive note.

- People don't "make" us mad and negative circumstances don't "ruin our whole weekend." *We* do these things, based on our poor reactions to people and circumstances.

Organization and Consistency

D o you fully trust your co-worker who has a cluttered desk and constantly searches for important papers that have been misplaced? Neither do I. Creating an organized system for dealing with the mountains of physical information we all need to do our jobs leads to consistency and reliability. Being able to find things quickly and track projects effectively leads to consistent productivity and engenders respect and appreciation from our colleagues. The trust we build, in turn, helps us continue to advance in the organization.

I will be the first to admit that I was a disorganized mess in my first management role! Organizational skills are not taught in school so many of us have had to figure out our own systems to keep track of various things. If you are like I was earlier in my career, then you have a bunch of yellow sticky notes in every conceivable place, multiple to-do lists (both written and electronic) and many slivers of paper, napkins, or envelopes with scribbled reminders.

I want to share with you some of the simple things that helped me become more organized as a manager, hoping that you can implement whichever ideas may be useful to you. I tend to be a bit old-school, so as you read be aware that most of this can also be digitally implemented. I just prefer paper copies for easier access and less electronic digging. If you are already an organized pro, just skip this chapter and please email me any suggestions you'd like to share! I can always improve.

Paper! What the heck do we do with all this paper? I thought computers would take most of it away, but I find there are still things I prefer in paper form. What works for me for organizing paper is utilizing file folders. When I find myself with a stack of papers that need a home, I grab a handful of file folders and, as I go through the stack, items get put into folders to be filed in my filing cabinet. If you work completely on a computer and your desktop is a mess of file icons, create folders right on your desktop and sort accordingly. Think about what you frequently leave unfiled. Typical file folders might include:

- To-Do
- Staff Meeting Notes
- Articles to Read
- Ideas
- Pending Sales
- Speeches

My To-Do file might contain yellow sticky notes, index cards on which I listed tasks when I woke up in the middle of the night, napkins with a to-do item listed and other random, task-related notes. At the end of each day, I consolidate these random notes onto one list (written on a simple, lined note pad) and I throw away all the other papers. Sometimes, when work is very busy, I categorize this main list by client or event. At times I have both a work and personal to-do list with subcategories. The list is organized based on what makes the most sense for me that week or month.

When I get very busy and begin to feel overwhelmed, I practice "triage," a medical term that means assigning degrees of urgency to wounded or ill patients. I take out my list and find the few items that I absolutely must finish by the end of the day (the "patients" in need of the most urgent care). Then I number those items in order of priority on my list. I focus on starting my day tackling those items in that order and, if I get sidetracked, I continue to coax myself back to this list. After I finish them, I choose the three most important items of those that remain, number them 1, 2, and 3, and begin to work through those. If I finish any more than those few initial items, I celebrate that everything else I do is icing on the cake. Focusing on only a few items at a time takes away the overwhelm that results from looking at a long, daunting list.

I take my Articles to Read file and a highlighter when traveling by plane, and I often have a copy of the electronic version in my computer in a folder called Articles, with subfolders labeled by topic. After I've read and highlighted the article, I file it in the most appropriate folder – maybe for an upcoming speech, for a workshop PowerPoint I'm creating, or for a client I'll be seeing soon. The Admin folder contains administrative information (processes or procedures or checklists for the office), and the Staff Meeting Notes folder has agendas, handouts, and notes from those meetings.

Clients often tell me they don't know what to do with themselves when they have downtime. I always suggest they work on leadership activities (what Stephen Covey labels Not Urgent but Very Important tasks in his 7 Habits book[6]). These items, which take time now for a payoff later, might include strategic/project planning, creating efficiencies, training/coaching others, or pursuing a new long-term project. My Ideas folder contains random papers listing ideas I'd like to implement when I have time, and I go to this folder and think about and/or work on these ideas when time permits.

The Pending Sales folder contains follow-up information or notes from initial meetings with people who want my help. Once they become a client, they get their own folders. I label a general folder with the company name for leadership team meeting notes I will take and then label individual folders with the name of each person I will coach. The general and individual folders are stored in either an accordion folder or in a bag with handles that I will take to the client site for meetings, so everything is stored in the same place.

My Speeches folder contains proposals I've sent to speak at national conferences and a spreadsheet of those I've accepted with information about each engagement. Once I'm approved to give a speech, a new file folder is created and labeled with the organization and date of the speech. I file the proposal in there along with a printed copy of the acceptance email and/or speaker contract, which often lists deadlines and other critical information. The file folder goes into an expandable (accordion) folder with all my current upcoming speeches, as well as the Speeches main folder.

As a side note, when I receive the speaker contract, I go to my calendar and record any due dates associated with the speech. I save time on my calendar for working on the PowerPoint and preparing other documents requested, scheduling the travel, hotel and rental car, and noting the travel dates for the speech itself. As I make airline, hotel and rental car reservations, I print the reservation information and put it in the folder for that particular speech. All of this can be put in online file folders as well. I have found it's more convenient to have paper copies I can access quickly and read/highlight when traveling without opening my laptop.

I realize you will not have the same names of folders I do, because you have a different job. My hope is that these examples help you generate ideas of how you might better organize your work using a simple file folder system. I used to resist filing things away, preferring multiple items on my desk at one time and trying to multi-task among the various papers and projects. Once I organized things into appropriately labeled file folders and consolidated my to-do list into one place where I could prioritize the tasks, I no longer had to see things in front of me to remember to work on them.

I've conversed with many of my clients about the inefficiencies of multi-tasking, but people continue to believe that it's effective. In the book *The Organized Mind* by Daniel J. Levitin, the author says "Our brains evolved to focus on one thing at a time... To pay attention to one thing means that we don't pay attention to something else. Attention is a limited-capacity resource."[7] Therefore, we get in trouble when driving and also using our hands (and mind) for other things, like eating or putting on lipstick or using our phone.

Our brains are not doing two things at once but, instead, are flitting back and forth between two things requiring our attention. These frequent switches come at a cognitive cost, and there are more things than ever in our world demanding our attention. According to Levitin, there are health benefits to learning new things, which we do by taking in all the information available to us in today's busy world. Because of this, learning systems to organize all this information becomes paramount.

I mentioned earlier that I often write to-do items on random slips of paper, napkins or envelopes and then consolidate them into a written list. Levitin found, while working on his book, that many executives, including those in high-tech industries, carried around implements for taking physical notes. Efficiency expert and author David Allen who wrote Getting Things Done advocates for what he calls "clearing the mind."[8] It's an exercise of getting things out of your head so your thinking of these random things won't distract you from focusing on your true priorities. To do this, find ways to write down what's in your head. You can take notes electronically or physically on paper. The point is to get these thoughts out of your head and captured on a list.

Many years ago, I felt overwhelmed regularly, and I would wake up in the night thinking of all the things I needed to get done. I would have difficulty going back to sleep because I was filled with worry that if I did, I would forget these important tasks. Instead, I would lie awake and repeat these to-do items in my mind over and over, in an attempt to memorize them. Cognitive psychologists call this thinking repetition the "rehearsal loop,"[9] which is an adapted behavior from pre-historic times when there were no ways of easily recording thoughts. Back then, we had to largely rely on our memory, so we would rehearse our thoughts to remember important things. It was possible to do so because cavemen were not bombarded with the overstimulated environments and information overload we experience today, which requires the expenditure of much more cognitive energy.

When I would experience the challenge of not being able to fall back asleep because of my thoughts, I forced myself out of bed to a stack of index cards and a pen I kept in the bathroom. With the light on low, so my husband wouldn't wake, I would jot down the thoughts I was having. Comforted that forgetting was no longer a threat, I went back to sleep easily. I still do this practice today, when needed, but have found that if I keep an accurate and current to-do list, I don't have tasks floating around in my head. They are already on paper, safe from my forgetfulness.

Email management can also produce great efficiency. I use a system David Allen introduces in his book Getting Things Done. Because new methods of managing electronic information will continue to be developed, I won't go into great detail about this system. Simply, I take Allen's advice to determine what to do with email as soon as it arrives, which he boils down into these four choices:

1) Do it (if the action required takes two minutes or less), then delete or archive it
2) Defer it (if it must be done by you and takes more than two minutes)
3) Delegate it (if someone else can do it)
4) Delete it.[10]

When I'm extremely busy, I only check email a few times a day. This has kept me from wasting an entire day responding to email (which I have done in the past). When my email is completely closed periodically, I can focus on what I'm doing without the distraction of a noise or visual telling me when messages arrive. If you find you keep your email open all day, just try to close it whenever you need to focus your attention on a tough mental task, like writing a report. Then open it back up when you finish. You'll probably find you haven't missed much! I have personally found, from practicing this, that I used to check my email way more than necessary.

Many of the things I've written about in this chapter lead to overall consistency and reliability. As a manager, we want people to be able to count on us consistently, and it's important to role model efficient and productive behavior. Having an organizational system to which you adhere will allow you to track important things, and that will increase your ability to meet deadlines and fulfill your promises.

Pro Tip from John Palmer, Director of Media and Public Relations at The Ohio Hospital Association

To be early is to be on time, to be on time is to be late, and to be late is inexcusable. I utilize my Outlook calendar to build in travel time, preparation time, debriefing time, etc. to ensure my schedule is successful and not chaotic. Your reputation is immediately developed based on simple behaviors such as preparedness, early arrival, tardiness, participation, contribution, and support. I make strong efforts to be an active team player within my department and company to help get projects completed.

Chapter Two – Key Points

- Being able to find things quickly and track projects effectively leads to consistent productivity.

- Organize paper by utilizing (physical or electronic) file folders.

- Consolidate random notes into one to-do list and throw away the other papers.

- When you feel overwhelmed, practice "triage" - prioritize your top three to-do items and do them first. If you finish before the end of the day, prioritize the next three and do them in order. Continue in this fashion, so you are doing highest priority items first each day.

- File folders you might consider:

    o Articles to Read - to read when you have down time

    o Ideas - for creative things you'd like to implement when you have time

    o Pending Sales - follow-up information or notes from initial meetings with people who want your help

    o Speeches - proposals sent to speak at national conferences

- Multi-tasking is inefficient and comes at a cognitive cost

- David Allen, author of Getting Things Done advocates for finding ways to write down what's in your head, what he calls "clearing the mind," so your thinking of random things won't distract you from focusing on your true priorities.

- Cognitive psychologists call the repeated ruminating we do the "rehearsal loop." In ancient times, we had to rely on our memory, so we would rehearse our thoughts to remember important things. Today, we can make time to jot down our thoughts through journaling or keeping to-do lists to free up cognitive energy.

- To manage email, author David Allen suggests choosing one of four options when an email arrives: 1) Do it (if the action required takes two minutes or less), then delete or archive it; 2) Defer it (if it must be done by you and takes more than two minutes); 3) Delegate it (if someone else can do it), or 4) Delete it.

CHAPTER THREE

Creating a Plan to Achieve Goals

———————○———————

I have found throughout my career that if I don't set goals with deadlines, things simply don't get done. Most of us have heard of SMART goals - they are Specific (answers the questions what, where, why, who, and which), Measurable (you can see the progress toward the goal), Achievable (is it realistic for you?), Relevant (is it worth doing? does it matter?), and Timely (by when will you achieve it?).[11]

An example of a SMART goal is to hire four people in the marketing division by the end of the year. It's specific - I'm hiring four people. It's measurable - I will know if I have or have not hired four people in the time frame I allotted. It's achievable - there are people available to hire and the time frame in which to do so is reasonable. It's relevant - I need to hire people to achieve my department's goals. It's timely - I have assigned a deadline.

I believe to achieve SMART goals, we should strive to be GREAT. To be GREAT you need:

- Guts – Courage, nerve, bravery. You must risk the possibility of failure.

- Repetition – By practicing long-term, we achieve goals.

- Effort – Drive, resolve, persistence in the face of adversity.

- Accountability – Tell others your goals for maximum self-accountability.

- Thoughts – What does your inner voice tell you? Thoughts dictate our behavior.

To be GREAT at achieving goals, it's important to have the guts to convert our nebulous dreams into time-bound, concrete goals. The reason many dreams aren't realized is that they have no deadline, so we don't plan for them. If your goal is to travel, make it more concrete by saying, "I want to travel to (fill in place) by (fill in date)." Now you're in a position to plan your action steps to achieve that goal. Action steps may include saving money, asking a friend/spouse if they'd like to go, making reservations on a plane/ship/train, and buying things to take on the trip. This takes guts because you are now accountable to the success or failure of achieving the goal.

One thing that helps goal achievement is repetition. A college professor of mine many years ago said, "Repetition is the key to learning." I have found that to be very true. Having a process to follow that can be replicated over and over goes a long way toward reaching goals. Achieving goals takes effort. It's typically not comfortable or easy. We have to take action, even when we are afraid, to move something forward. The more we do something, the easier and more comfortable it becomes.

Project management, succession planning, and strategic planning all work in much the same way. We must know what the end goal is and then map out the action steps we'll take to get there in the time allotted. Goals can feel overwhelming until we break them up into smaller, manageable pieces that can be accomplished over a period of time. Resist the temptation to wallow in overwhelm just so you don't have to risk failure. Without this risk, you can't succeed.

Accountability is also a key factor in being GREAT at achieving goals. There is no single right way to organize tasks, but two good ways I have found to ensure goal achievement are: 1) choosing a physical (as opposed to mental) method of keeping track of tasks so you can assess progress and 2) having an accountability partner.

Some of my clients (especially in the construction industry) keep to-do items in their head (mentally), as opposed to on paper (physically). It doesn't work well. There's simply too much to remember these days. To track tasks, I recommend utilizing a note-taking method, such as an electronic notepad on your cell phone, 3x5 cards, or a physical pad of paper or notebook. Keep it with you to track to-do items as they come up. When we receive verbal requests, there is no written account of what people have asked of us, so these items are more likely to fall through the cracks. It's mentally taxing to have to catalog all our tasks mentally, so keeping a physical list takes this mental burden away.

As an executive coach, I am a built-in accountability partner for my clients, but there are ways to keep yourself and your colleagues or friends accountable without hiring outside help. Having an accountability partner who is working toward the same goal can be very beneficial. Once, a client told me that he and his friend were committed to working out together. To ensure that they showed up to every workout, they wrote each other a check for $500 with the understanding that if the other person didn't show up for a workout, they could cash the check. They were very motivated to keep their commitment to each other!

Someone with a different goal can also help, if you mutually agree to help each other stay accountable to these different goals. I have two friends I go to dinner with monthly. Many years ago, we decided at one of our dinners that we'd like to help one another achieve a goal. We each chose a goal and at our monthly dinners, we checked in with one another on progress toward our goals. The writing of my first book, *Shut Up and Lead*, came out of that effort. It's amazing what you can achieve when you know someone will be checking in on your progress regularly.

If you don't have others to help you, self-accountability can be very tricky. We are great at procrastinating and rationalizing why it's okay that something didn't happen. What I do for self-accountability is schedule things on my calendar and make a personal commitment to doing whatever appears there. If I want to work out three times a week, I write it on my calendar so it will happen. Another method I use for self-accountability is telling other people about my goal. Doing this puts a bit more pressure on myself because I know people will ask about my progress, not realizing they are part of my accountability system.

The last step in being GREAT is controlling our thoughts. If you have a harsh inner critic, it can be tough to reach your goals. Step one is hearing that internal voice. Some of my clients work at such a fast, constant pace that they don't have periods of mental rest when they can tune in to what they are saying to themselves internally. Step two is changing the message, if all you are hearing is criticism.

If you had a supervisor at work who criticized you all day, would you feel excited to work even harder or depressed and ready to give up? We are fully in control of our thoughts, but we must first recognize what they are. If they sound like a criticizing supervisor, then we can decide what we'd like them to be instead. Once we decide that, we have to practice this new healthy thinking, so we are motivated to achieve goals. The repetition of positive, motivational thoughts is self-coaching. We have this ability 24 hours a day; we just need to exercise it.

Pro Tip from Mary Garrick, Vice President of Brand and Creative, Upward Brand Interactions

Are you motivated by problem solving or goal setting? When it comes to motivating your team, and yourself, it's important to recognize the dichotomy between those who have a goal-setting mindset and a problem-solving mindset. People who are motivated by setting goals tend to be focused on the future and big picture thinking, while those who are motivated by solving problems focus more on the present situation and the details pertinent to the solution. Twenty percent of the population are goal oriented, while the remainder are problem solvers. Understanding how to frame up your goal, or problem, based on each person's inclination can make a huge difference in motivating your team.

Chapter Three – Key Points

- SMART goals are Specific (answers the questions what, where, why, who, and which), Measurable (you can see the progress toward the goal), Achievable (is it realistic for you?), Relevant (is it worth doing? does it matter?), and Timely (by when will you achieve it?).

- To achieve SMART goals, strive to be GREAT. You will need:

    o Guts – Courage, nerve, bravery.

    o Repetition – Long-term practice.

    o Effort – Drive, resolve, persistence.

    o Accountability – Tell others your goals.

    o Thoughts – Thoughts dictate our behavior.

- The reason many dreams aren't realized is that they have no deadline, so we don't plan for them.

- Goals can feel overwhelming, so break them up into smaller, manageable pieces that can be accomplished over a period of time.

- Two good ways to ensure goal achievement are: 1) choosing a physical (as opposed to mental) method of keeping track of tasks so you can assess progress and 2) having an accountability partner.

- For self-accountability, schedule things on your calendar and make a personal commitment to doing whatever appears there.

- To control our thoughts when we are self-criticizing, we must first recognize what they are. We can then decide what we'd like them to be instead. Once we decide that, we have to practice, with repetition, the positive, motivational thoughts. This is self-coaching.

Section Two: Encourage Excellence

"Good leadership consists of showing average people how to do the work of superior people."

- John D. Rockefeller

Hiring and Onboarding Employees

———— o ————

S hifting our focus from ourselves to the employees we will work with, we'll start at the beginning by making sure we're bringing the right people onboard. Many staffing mistakes happen in the hiring phase. People look so good on paper, and they say all the right things in the interview. Then we are shocked when we hire them, and they can't do what they say they can do.

When hiring, I always think about trust. How can we trust someone to work hard and do what they say they will do? In his book *The Speed of Trust: The One Thing That Changes Everything*, Stephen M.R. Covey reveals that trust comes from both character and competence.[12] During the hiring process, it's important to assess both because trust is essential in the workplace.

Competence seems easier to assess in the interview process. We not only have references from the candidate, but we also can test the person's knowledge and capabilities right there during the interview. I worked with a client who consistently hired candidates who said they could do the work and, upon hiring them, found they could not. Going through this hiring exercise only to let the person go is extremely costly. The U.S. Department of Labor puts the price tag of a bad hire at 30 percent (or more) of the employee's first-year earnings.[13]

There are several things you can do to help ensure you're choosing a competent person:

Take Your Time. Many people make poor hiring decisions because of their need to fill the job quickly. When enticed to make the choice to be expedient over thorough, remember the cost in staff time and energy on the back end. If you hire quickly and end up having to fire the person, you waste a lot of resources by training and onboarding them. You also jeopardize the cohesiveness of the team by introducing a frustrating element right when they are desperate for help. Finally, you have to start the entire process over, which takes much more time than just doing it right the first time. The adage "haste makes waste" couldn't be truer than in the hiring process.

Check References. Hiring managers often think candidates will only give you positive references. I have been surprised when I ask, "Would you hire this person again?" and hear that they would not. It's always worth it to make the call. I often call past employers (not the company they are leaving) even if they don't appear on the candidate's list of references. If I know someone at the company because they're in my industry, I'll start with a call to that person. I usually get the most helpful information from someone who's not in human resources and is giving me candid feedback as an industry friend.

Test Them. If you want to ensure someone can do the task they say they can do on their resume, devise a dummy test for them to prove themselves. You can create these tests to assess hard skills like math, writing, or industry knowledge. If the job requires high-level thinking or planning, ask candidates to respond to scenarios and observe how they think or address the problem. Some of these may not have one "right" answer, but their answer can be used to learn more about what kind of co-worker, leader, or decision maker they are.

Invite Objectivity. We often ask candidates to interview with those who will be supervising them or working in the same department. One tactic to ensure objectivity is to invite someone who will have a tangential relationship with the new employee to be part of the interview process. This person will often give important, unbiased insight because they are less focused on hard skills and more focused on overall cultural fit.

To assess character in the hiring process is more complicated. One's character is the expression of one's values, such as integrity, loyalty, respectfulness, and accountability. Experience is obvious, but understanding character requires vulnerability from the candidate, and not everyone feels comfortable sharing personal information with someone they just met. We must ask difficult questions to glean this information, such as:

- How do you define and deal with difficult co-workers?

- Tell me about a time when you failed. How did you handle that?

- Tell me about a time you faced adversity. How did you react?

- What do you see as the pros and cons of having a diverse workplace?

- How would your best friend describe your personality?

Our company's president usually shares our company values with candidates and asks which of the values resonates most with them and why. We learn a great deal about a candidate from just that one question.

When interviewing, I listen carefully to how they talk about the possibility of working with me. Some candidates express excitement over what they will learn in the role, how the job will prepare them for the future, and the great benefits they will receive. In other words, it's all about them and what they will get. Others frame their comments around what skills they can bring to our workplace, how they will positively influence the culture, and ideas they have to impact the company's bottom line. It's all about us and what they will give. Candidates rarely do this strategically; they are simply sharing their thoughts. I would much rather hire someone who thinks of the team before themselves.

Another way to ensure you have a person of good character is to conduct a background check. Many people lie on their resumes, and while some of these are little embellishments, others are serious lies that will affect trust and perhaps even job performance. If the candidate is applying for a prominent role, dealing with large amounts of money, or privy to private employee information, it would be wise to consider conducting a background check on their financial, personal, and/or criminal history.

Once you've found a suitable employee, onboarding can be challenging. We are all so busy doing our jobs that worrying about whether or not a new employee feels welcome can be daunting, especially if you work in a smaller office where there are no designated human resources personnel.

To effectively onboard someone, take time in the interview to get to know some personal things about them. You can ask what they like to do for fun, if they have a favorite sport to watch, or a favorite vacation spot. You can also ask how best they learn - by listening and watching while someone shows them how to perform a task, by writing the steps of a process down and then practicing with their notes, by physically doing the task with someone talking them through it, by seeing a visual depiction of a process or example of a finished product, or perhaps another way. This will help you decide the most effective way to train the person for the job.

Here are some things you may consider doing in preparation for their first day of work:

- Order their business cards (send them a proof to make sure their name and credentials are listed as they'd like)

- Order a nameplate for their desk or door (if appropriate)

- Schedule training time

- Compile all the forms they will need to fill out (benefits, retirement accounts, taxes)

- Schedule time to fill out forms and meet with an HR person

- Print or create an updated employee or policy handbook

- Order office equipment (computer, phone, filing cabinet)

- Order desk supplies (pens, paper, stapler, scissors, file folders, etc.)

- When the new employee arrives, you may:

- Welcome them and lead them to their desk, filled with new supplies and equipment. Ask them to let you know if they need additional supplies.

- Have a welcome basket waiting for them that features items they might like such as:

- o   A hat with the logo of a local sports team

- o   A gift card to a nearby restaurant

- o   A welcome card signed by co-workers

- o   Marketing giveaway items, like shirts or pens featuring the company logo

- Arrange for a screensaver on their computer of their favorite sports team or vacation spot. You can also pick them out a mousepad they might like.

- Leave a schedule on their desk for their first few days that details any training, time to fill out forms, if someone's taking them to lunch, meetings they must attend, time to be introduced to colleagues, and a meeting with their supervisor at the end of the day to answer questions.

- If it's a big office, leave a map on their desk.

- Leave them a file folder of important checklists or processes from the previous employee, and an organizational chart or list of employee phone extensions.

One thing that troubles many managers I coach is that they are expected to train new employees (or delegate the task to one of the new-hire's co-workers) when they have had no instruction about how to teach other adults. In addition, people on the team are typically dealing with a heavy workload, which is why they've hired someone. It's common to feel resentment about training when you need the new person to learn quickly so they can help ease the workload burden. Remember, time spent here will save you time later.

There are two things you can do to make the process of training more effective: teach the employee in the manner in which they learn best, and practice empathy and patience. If you've asked your new hire how they best learn in the interview process, confirm that preference with them. Some people are nervous in the interview and may not remember what they said.

Remember what it was like when you were new to a job. Not everyone learns at the same pace, so be patient. Know that when people are stressed, it's harder for them to think clearly. The first few days on a new job are stressful, so check in with the new employee frequently to assess understanding. Be clear about your expectations. If you expect to show them something once and not have to show them again, be sure to say this and invite them to take notes so they will have a written process to follow next time. Handouts of processes or rules also help, and it takes pressure off the trainer to go over these things.

If the new employee is to read training manuals or watch instructional videos, schedule time for this. Tell them to let you know when they're done and that you will ask them questions to assess their learning. By laying out this expectation, they are much more likely to listen intently or read carefully. Remember to ask them questions when they let you know they have finished. If they can't answer correctly, you may ask them to review the material again to ensure learning.

During the training process, give the new employee lots of positive reinforcement. Catch them doing things right and tell them specifically what you like.[14] For example, "I really appreciate that you have been on time for all our meetings. That's something I value." When you praise specifically, you will see more of that behavior you've called out. It's much more effective than general praise such as, "Good job today!" Praise their effort to learn. You might say, "I saw you re-reading the section of the employee manual you asked questions about. I am impressed by your effort to learn this material." Invite them to ask frequent questions. Having to learn new things while trying to fit in with an established team is daunting, so praise and support goes a long way in helping them feel hopeful that they can form healthy relationships and contribute in a meaningful way.

Pro Tip from Bill Patton, Director of Operations at Thompson Concrete

I highly recommend taking the time to plan and personalize early interactions with new employees. In an effort to personalize our onboarding procedure, I've tried a few different things. I sent an email to a new employee a day before she started, expressing excitement that she would be joining us, telling her how much I enjoyed working at the company, and asking if she had any questions I could answer in advance of her first day. It was a good icebreaker that she seemed to appreciate.

In another case, I met a new employee on our front porch. I introduced him to coworkers who escorted him down to the yard where he was introduced to his crew. We checked in with him at the end of the day to see how everything went and followed up daily thereafter. Although this employee ended up pursuing a career in a completely different industry, he pulled me off to the side before leaving to tell me how much he appreciated his treatment and that he felt as if he were part of the team from day one. I am surprised at how just a little advanced planning and a few thoughtful communications can be so meaningful. Onboarding presents a great opportunity to make a new employee feel like they are part of the family from the first minute they arrive.

Chapter Four – Key Points

- When hiring, consider trust. According to Stephen M.R. Covey, and outlined in his book *The Speed of Trust*, trust is made up of character (expression of values) and competence (knowledge and capabilities).

- The U.S. Department of Labor puts the price tag of a bad hire at 30 percent (or more) of the employee's first-year earnings.

- To ensure a candidate's competence:
  - Take your time in hiring
  - Check references
  - Test them in area of competence you seek
  - Invite objectivity by allowing those of other departments to take part in the interviewing process

- To ensure a candidate has good character:
  - Ask difficult questions to understand the person's values and morals
  - Share your company's values and ask what resonates with them
  - Listen carefully to how they talk about what they will get or give if they are selected for the job
  - Conduct a background check

- To effectively onboard a new hire, take time in the interview to get to know some personal things about them and how they best learn.

- To prepare for an employee's first day of work, order supplies, schedule training time, compile forms they will need to complete, secure an updated employee or policy handbook, and order office equipment.

- Personalize some items to welcome the employee on his or her first day and leave information and training agendas on the desk.

- To make the process of training more effective: teach the employee in the manner in which they learn best, practice empathy and patience, be clear about your expectations, and give positive reinforcement as they learn.

CHAPTER FIVE

Healthy Team Dynamics

As I mentioned in this book's introduction, we are hard-wired for connection. Being mindful of appropriate workplace conduct, we can find ways to raise the levels of the hormone oxytocin in our employees. Oxytocin encourages trust, combats feelings of depression, causes us to feel empathy, and motivates us to seek connection and support.

Although this hormone is naturally released, there are specific things we can do to stimulate the hormone purposefully. In his book *The Moral Molecule*, scientist Paul Zak offers multiple ways to raise oxytocin (based on measuring changes in oxytocin levels in human blood).[15]

1. Tell others you love or appreciate them.
2. Pet a dog or cat.
3. Ride a roller coaster with a friend. (Activities that are moderately stressful and done with someone else raises oxytocin levels.)

4. Use social media. (100% of the people Dr. Zak tested using social media had an increase in oxytocin.)

5. Meditate while focusing on others. (Dr. Zak's lab found that a form of meditation called "metta," in which one focuses on loving others, is better at fostering social connections than standard mindfulness meditation.)

6. Share a meal. (Moderate eating calms us and helps us bond with others.)

7. Give someone a gift.

8. Listen with your eyes. (When you're with someone, give them your full attention.)

We feel so good when we help others because we are supposed to! It's why we are here on earth - for connection. It's why we are driven to help others succeed in the workplace. It positively impacts us when we positively impact others.

We are currently living in what the writer George Monbiot has called "the age of loneliness," where people are more removed from human connection than ever before.[16] In business, we used to talk about getting "face-time" with someone, which meant being in the same room, having a conversation, and truly connecting. Now, FaceTime is an app which, although a step up from a telephone conversation, still leaves out important body language, dress, and environmental clues about the person. We live online, communicating with "friends" we may have never met and/or know little about, or posting photos of our shining moments in life, leaving out all the crummy or dull moments that make up the other 95% of our lives.

To build healthy workplace relationships, we need to truly connect with others. True connection requires vulnerability, authenticity, and the willingness to risk looking stupid, making mistakes, and being wrong. Many managers and leaders think that their role dictates they must 1) be knowledgeable about everything in their industry and 2) make the "right" decisions (those that will work perfectly, as planned). That's a lot of pressure that leads to an incredibly unhealthy work environment because we don't want others to learn that we don't know everything and may make faulty decisions.

First, we can't know everything in our field because of the sheer volume of information being discovered and shared at breakneck speed. Even though you may be an avid reader of industry materials, a multitude of writers are out there writing mountainous piles of more material. It's a sad impossibility that we will ever be able to read everything we want to in our lifetime.

Second, leaders and managers rarely have all the information they'd like with which to make a decision by the time a deadline arrives. Thus, we often must decide with much less than 100% of the information out there. When staff members beg me, in our executive coaching sessions, to persuade their CEO into telling them what he will do next, I often smile because I get the same answer repeatedly from leaders in various industries. My conversation with the CEO goes like this:

"Your staff members are dying to hear your decision. Can you share with them what you plan to do next?"

"I honestly don't know."

"Okay, then just tell them you don't know."

"I can't do that. I'm *supposed* to know. They *expect* me to know."

Are leaders ever allowed to be indecisive, procrastinate or worry about a decision? Are they allowed to be confused? I say yes. In fact, it's normal. Because we can't know anything 100%, we need others to share thoughts and information. This is especially true when the stakes are high. The best decision is made with the highest percentage of information available to us. And yet I continue to see leaders who think they must make decisions alone.

Every decision is a risk, especially at the top of a company, which is why decision making is such a vulnerable, and sometimes scary, activity. I think it's imperative that leaders and managers embrace the fact that they won't always have the answers and become more comfortable with telling people they don't know yet and need more time to decide. And it would help if they also accepted that sometimes deciding promptly may mean not being positive the decision will be "right," or will go as planned.

Vulnerability, although uncomfortable, leads to connection and trust. Connection is the key to building healthy workplace relationships. If you are managing a team of competitive overachievers, find ways for them to connect. You might:

- Pair people on projects so they experience not only the openness needed for collaboration but also sharing credit when they succeed.

- Create processes that require interdependence, so team members learn the importance of relying on one another to accomplish goals.

- Periodically throw a get-to-know-you exercise in your team meetings, so colleagues can learn more about one another on a personal level.

- Invite two direct reports to lunch and ask questions that allow all three of you to better understand one another.

- Take a staff meeting field trip to a nearby park, allowing the team a more casual, open format in which to share ideas.

As you attempt to foster connection on your team, it's also important to consider where to set boundaries. There are many differing views on how close to allow yourself to get with colleagues. In the event one of you are promoted to a position where one will supervise the other, it can be difficult for the supervisor to keep the other person accountable. If you find yourself in this situation, I suggest having a clear conversation with your direct report to manage expectations. Explain that your new role requires that you keep them accountable despite your previous relationship as peers and that you plan to treat them, at work, as you would any of your other direct reports. Being this person's supervisor will challenge your assertiveness, so give thought to how you will be fair and clear with all direct reports.

Tom Rath, author of *How Full Is Your Bucket?*, and Barry Conchie, coauthor of *Strengths Based Leadership*, write that strong teams "are often characterized by healthy debate and at times, heated arguments. What distinguishes strong teams from dysfunctional ones is that debate doesn't cause them to fragment. Instead of becoming more isolated during tough times, these teams actually gain strength and develop cohesion."[17]

Being fair and clear may result in challenging discussions. The willingness to have these difficult discussions, if entertained with openness and curiosity, will result in team cohesion and understanding. If you set aside all assumptions and are open to considering the facts available and the opinions of others, these discussions often result in healthier workplace relationships.

Pro Tip from Donna Stevens, Vice President Human Resources at Matesich Distributing Co.

There was a time when we were bringing in a new team manager because the person managing that team (a member of management staff) was also managing another department and working on several large projects for the company. With everything that was going on, performance reviews for the team had fallen behind, and since it was common practice at that time to grant pay increases based on their performance reviews, they didn't receive those on time either.

We had an employee in that department, who worked a position that was hard to fill and did it very well. She had been due for a review in February, and it was now September. I wanted her to receive a pay increase in recognition of her efforts, so I asked the new manager to write a review, and we gave her a pay increase, including $750 in retroactive pay. The employee was very upset (to the point of tears) and questioned how this manager could possibly write a review for her when she knew nothing about her job or performance.

So, my desire to do something that should have made her happy had the opposite effect. Had I taken the time to think it through, I might have realized that the review would be meaningless, and not only of little value to the employee, but an insult. What I should have done was continue to remind/urge the manager responsible to get it done, or at the very least just convince him to give her the pay increase she earned.

Just because it's the right thing to do, doesn't mean it's the right thing to do.

Chapter Five – Key Points

- The naturally released hormone oxytocin encourages trust, combats feelings of depression, causes us to feel empathy, and motivates us to seek connection and support.

- We can deliberately produce oxytocin, to help our work team connect, by telling someone we appreciate them, meditating while focusing on others, sharing a meal, giving someone a gift, or listening intently.

- To build healthy workplace relationships, we need to truly connect with others, which requires vulnerability, authenticity, and the willingness to risk looking stupid, making mistakes, and being wrong.

- If leaders and managers embrace the fact that they won't always have the answers and become more comfortable with telling people they don't know, it will lead to connection and trust.

- To create trust and connection on your team:
    - Pair people on projects.
    - Create processes that require interdependence.
    - Periodically throw a get-to-know-you exercise in your team meetings.
    - Invite two direct reports to lunch and ask questions.
    - Take a staff meeting field trip to a nearby park.

- Set boundaries by having a clear conversation with your direct report to manage expectations about your work and personal relationship.

- The willingness to have difficult discussions, if entertained with openness and curiosity, will result in team cohesion and understanding.

CHAPTER SIX

Effective Communication

I wrote about assertive communication in my first book, *Shut Up and Lead: A Communicator's Guide to Quiet Leadership,* because I've struggled to overcome passive communication most of my adult life. Assertive communication takes place when a communicator is confident or courageous enough to ask for what they need or ask someone to stop behavior that is hurtful. In contrast, passive people want to feel loved so they do and say everything they can to preserve a relationship, even if the other person is taking advantage of them. On the other end of the communication spectrum, aggressive people seek to control others so they won't be hurt. If they are demanding and in control, then others can't get close enough to know them and potentially hurt them.

Early in my career, I was very passive. I was often overwhelmed, never told people no, was taken advantage of, and was scared to death to be honest about any negative feelings I harbored. Becoming more assertive has helped me become a better leader and manager, and this is something I continue to practice.

In this book's introduction, I said I would explain how changing my thinking started me on my life-altering path to more assertive behavior. When I began working at Integrated Leadership Systems in 2006, I learned to apply the principles of Cognitive Behavioral Therapy. CBT contends that our thoughts lead to emotional states that result in our behavior.[18] If we can identify thoughts that are unhelpful or unreasonable and change them to more productive thoughts, the emotion and behavior follow. If we are unhappy with our behavior, we start by changing our thoughts that ultimately produce that behavior.

More specifically, our negative thoughts or assumptions lead to negative emotions, which lead to unhelpful or dysfunctional behavior. In contrast, positive thoughts and assumptions lead to positive emotions and helpful or functional behavior. Our brain has been programmed throughout our lives (because of our unique experiences) to look for patterns so that we can interpret situations and make choices about how to behave. We are prone to making assumptions all day long based on the patterns our brain has identified.

Because of our unique experiences, we develop inimitable rules to live by, which become our core beliefs (the lens through which we view the world). We develop an internal monologue about the world that colors our interpretations and perceptions. The problem with conflict is that each person can only see through their own lens. The trick to communicating better with others is to recognize this and seek to understand the other person's perspective instead of just pushing ours on them. Nobody is "right;" we are all simply different.

We are capable of choosing the way we think, although few adults know or practice this. When we experience an unhealthy thought or make a negative assumption, we can pause and choose a new, more productive thought. This new thought will lead to a better emotion and more productive behavior. It takes time, cognitive energy, and patience to identify these thought patterns and become adept at overriding them with healthier thoughts. Over time though, our brain maps these new neural pathways until they become our new, healthy thinking habits.

In my case, passive, people-pleasing behavior was becoming a serious problem at both work and home. I was overwhelmed on a regular basis because I never said no. My thoughts that led to the behavior were many:

- I want everyone to like me. If they don't, I'm worthless.

- Conflict makes people dislike me.

- Saying no is un-Christian. Christians help others and are selfless.

- Saying no to friends and family means I will have no help when I need it.

- Sharing emotions is unnecessary. Nobody cares.

- I can do it all. Sleep is overrated.

These thoughts led primarily to the feeling of resentment. I also felt insignificant, unappreciated, insincere, scared, hurt and used. This damaging self-talk had to change. Once I acknowledged what I was thinking and how those thoughts made me feel, I went about changing them. The new statements I began to practice thinking were:

- It's unreasonable to think everyone will like me. Some people just won't. That's okay.

- Conflict can strengthen relationships if handled properly.

- God wants me to be happy and healthy. If I say yes too much, I am neither.

- My true friends and my family will always be there for me.

- Sharing emotions enhances relationships. People care; they're just afraid to be vulnerable.

- I have limits. I must take care of myself.

Practicing this new way of thinking led to better emotional states (optimistic, hopeful, excited), which resulted in more effective behavior. This process takes time and a lot of cognitive energy at the beginning. Once these new healthy thinking patterns become routine, the effort you once expended goes away. It has taken me years of practice to become more assertive, and the time spent has truly been worth it. Assertive behavior is absolutely essential to being an effective manager and leader.

In this chapter, I'd also like to cover more advanced concepts of communication that might aid readers in effectively leading and managing others. These concepts include Actor-Observer Bias, adjusting our preferences to better understand and relate to others, ways to foster empathy with those who are different from us, and recognizing cultural differences.

There is a social psychology principle called Actor-Observer Bias, wherein a person attributes their own behavior to external, situational causes but attributes other people's actions to internal causes.[19] For example, if I have high blood pressure, I'm likely to think of it as genetic (and, thus, out of my control). If my neighbor has high blood pressure, I'm likely to think it's because he eats too many jelly donuts and doesn't exercise (within his control). All of these factors (and more) can lead to high blood pressure. My biased thinking, however, exonerates myself but finds shortcomings with my neighbor. As you can imagine, Actor-Observer Bias often results in disagreement, assumptions and blaming.

Most people communicate in ways that best suit their own preference. If you prefer to communicate directly and state what you need, then you will likely employ this same communication method each time you communicate, without regard to the receiver's preference. If someone is offended by your communication style, you may wonder why and think they are too sensitive (a fixed personality trait), when in reality, your own communication style may be part of the problem.

To communicate with someone who is much more sensitive than I am, I will get better results if I adjust my communication style to meet them where they are emotionally. To ensure the receiver is more receptive, I can use a gentler style of communication. If I know feedback is tough for this sensitive person to hear, I may forego my direct communication style and, instead, begin our discussion with, "I'd like to give you some feedback about what I observed recently, and I'm worried it may upset you." In saying this, I am allowing them a moment to put on their emotional armor to prepare for the feedback I will give.

Trying this approach with someone who is comfortable with direct communication likely won't offend them, even though it may not be necessary. If you are not sure if they are sensitive, it's a safer choice to default to this gentle approach than to use a very direct approach. A more sensitive approach is acceptable in nearly all cases, whereas a direct approach may be unwelcomed in some.

Many people are resentful when asked to change their preferred communication style to be more sensitive. I've heard things like, "They need to toughen up." But it is with self-interest that we adjust our style to meet the needs of those with whom we communicate. In wanting to work more effectively with the listener, I should adjust my communication style to what works best for them, so I ultimately get what I need or want.

Managers often begin a difficult conversation with unhelpful baggage; namely the thought that they are "right," negative assumptions about the other person's intent, and the unwillingness to be vulnerable. When complicated situations arise, we often tell ourselves that the other person is wrong or to blame, especially if we are in a position of power or the more experienced of the pair. Conversely, the other person often thinks *we* are wrong or to blame. In reality, there is a part both communicators play in any disagreement. Because our perspective is biased in favor of ourselves, it's difficult to empathize with others.

In attempting to have a difficult conversation, it's healthy to approach the other person with empathy, recognizing that you both have unique perspectives. The point of the conversation is not to assess or discuss who's wrong or to blame, but to understand how the other person is thinking about the situation and to agree on how to move forward in a way both people accept.

Example: You are managing someone who always waits until the last minute to complete her work. You may have labeled her (in your head) as a lazy procrastinator. If you often follow up with your direct report as the deadline looms because of your anxiety, she may label you (in her head) a controlling micro-manager. Instead of approaching your direct report with resentment because of your negative assumption about her, you could, instead, approach her with curiosity about her perspective. Here's how that conversation might unfold, beginning with the supervisor:

"I've noticed that you often wait until just before a deadline to complete work. When this happens, I feel anxious. I worry that I won't get what I need on time. What's going on for you as a deadline approaches?"

"I didn't realize you were anxious. I plan out my work carefully, so if you don't need the document until Friday and I have other more urgent things to do during the week, I'll wait until Thursday afternoon to work on it. I always meet the deadline, so I'm not sure what the problem is."

"I guess I'm uncomfortable with that. What if an unexpected problem arises? You might not get the work done on time. This anxiety I feel often leads me to check in with you repeatedly as the deadline nears. I'm sure that drives you crazy."

"When you check in a lot, I feel untrusted and micro-managed. I've never missed a deadline, so your check-ins were very confusing. Again, I didn't realize you were anxious. If you're worried, just tell me a deadline that would make you more comfortable, like a day or two before you actually need it. Would that work?"

"Yes; maybe that will work. Let's try it."

What complicates communication further is the speed at which we deliver and receive messages today. We think email, texting, and posting online are excellent communication advancements, but I'm not convinced. How often have we hit send only to realize we forgot the attachment, copied someone we shouldn't have, or suspect we misunderstood what was said because these vehicles lack tone. Our expectation of how long it should take before someone responds has become ridiculous. Just today, in need of a quick answer to a question, I fired off an email. When I didn't get a response within ten minutes, I sent a follow-up text. I was about to call the person five minutes after sending the text when I mentally stepped back and considered my actions. If it was that urgent, I should have chosen the best communication tool (probably a phone call) at the beginning.

Instead of defaulting to the easiest way for us to communicate, why don't we use the most effective way? If someone is on a conference call, it's more effective for me to text them a question than to open the door to their office. When I want to schedule a meeting with someone, it may be more effective to call them instead of shooting dates back and forth over several emails. Upon receiving an electronic communication that doesn't sit well with me, it's better to call the sender or visit them in person to discuss it. Sometimes when reading text, we assume a negative tone that the sender may not have intended.

People often hide behind electronic communication. When I get what I perceive as an angry email or voicemail message and I address it in person, the sender is much calmer when they are standing in front of me. Many times, I find they are not angry at all. But if they were upset, we're more likely to have a reasonable conversation in person. It's easier to say nasty things electronically and more difficult to say those things directly to another person. Even with the geographically diverse teams with whom many of us work these days, there are plenty of free video conferencing options that, by letting us see the other person, allow us to gather non-verbal cues that help us communicate more clearly.

When I worked in a law firm many years ago, email was my default form of communication. Over time, I noticed that in response to my emails, some lawyers would come to my office to discuss the matter, others would call me in response, and still others would respond with an email. As I learned their preferred methods of communication, I began mirroring each person. If Joe always came to see me in person, I visited Joe in person instead of emailing. If Sue always called me on the phone to make a request, I called her if I needed help. These simple changes I made to communicate with them in the way it seemed they preferred went a long way toward bettering those relationships.

Another communication challenge we face is understanding cultural differences. For instance, in some cultures people nod just to show they are listening, not that they agree with you. In some cultures, the hierarchy is rather flat, so executives and leaders work collaboratively. Other cultures have many layers in the hierarchy so employees are only allowed to work with the level of leadership directly above them and may seldom be allowed an audience with senior staff. In addition, various cultures have diverse methods and time frames for approaching decision making. U.S. executives are seen as very swift decision makers compared to other cultures.[20] In a recent speech I gave at a conference for nurses, an audience member pointed out that what we think of as "good eye contact" to show interest and good listening skills is an affront in her culture. Although we may prize direct eye contact in the United States, it is not acceptable everywhere. Being cognizant of these differences helps us embrace the fact that people aren't doing things because they are rude or insulting, but because culture differences exist and can be confusing to all of us.

We can change our communication style regardless of our personal preferences. Although each of us has a definition of who we are, made up of all the experiences we've had throughout our lives, the connections in our brains continue to form and re-form as we learn new things and have new experiences.[21] It seems many people think the definition we hold of ourselves is finite and unchangeable, that it's part of their DNA or personality. That is not the case. We are capable of improving ourselves throughout our lifetime, and continuing to improve as communicators certainly enhances business relationships.

Pro Tip from Brian Ahern, Chief Influence Officer at Influence PEOPLE

Ask; don't tell. When you ask and people say "Yes," they are far more likely to follow through as opposed to when being told. It triggers the principle of consistency, which highlights people's desire to be consistent in word and deed.

Chapter Six – Key Points

- Cognitive Behavioral Therapy (CBT) contends that our thoughts lead to emotional states that result in our behavior. If we can identify thoughts that are unhelpful and change them to more productive thoughts, the emotion and behavior follow.

- Our negative thoughts or assumptions lead to negative emotions, which lead to unhelpful or dysfunctional behavior.

- We have conflict because each person can only see through his or her own lens. To communicate better with others, we must seek to understand the other person's perspective instead of just pushing ours on them.

- It takes time, cognitive energy, and patience to identify unhelpful thoughts and become adept at overriding them with healthier thoughts. Over time though, our brain maps these new neural pathways until they become our new, healthy thinking habits.

- Actor-Observer Bias is when a person attributes their own behavior to external, situational causes but attributes other people's actions to internal causes. This often results in disagreement, assumptions and blaming.

- To communicate with someone who is much more sensitive, adjust your communication style to meet them where they are emotionally. Think about how they will receive your message instead of how you prefer to deliver it.

- When entering a difficult conversation, approach the other person with empathy, recognizing that you both have unique perspectives. The point of the conversation is to understand how the other person is thinking about the situation and to agree on how to move forward in a way both people accept.

- Instead of defaulting to the easiest way to communicate, take time to consider the most effective way.

- Avoid hiding behind electronic communication. When you get what you perceive as an angry email or voicemail message, address it in person.

- Being cognizant of cultural differences helps us understand that people aren't doing things because they are rude or insulting, but because these differences exist and can be confusing to all of us.

- Our current definition of ourselves is not part of our DNA. We are capable of improving ourselves throughout our lifetime, and our continued improvement enhances business relationships.

Sustainable Accountability

T he two biggest challenges I see in almost every client organization are communication (which we have already covered) and accountability. Holding others accountable is a long process that involves building trust, and communication is a very big component of doing it effectively.

To discover if you can trust them to do what they say they will do, it's important to delegate appropriately. By this I mean that early on, give the person small, manageable tasks you are fairly certain they can do with little guidance. As they show you they can meet your expectations of the deliverable and meet deadlines, you can challenge them with progressively more difficult tasks. If at any point they are not meeting your expectations, it's time for a conversation and possibly additional training. If they exceed your expectations, let them know they have. At that point, you may want to let them take ownership of entire projects or processes.

When you begin working with a direct report, especially one you have inherited (not one you have hired), you may not have a sense of that person's level of productivity and reliability. It is important to establish an employee's ideal workload so that you have a benchmark against which to hold them accountable.

I have learned through the years that people have different workload capacities. If you worked on a factory assembly line, for example, you would see that some people can make 500 widgets in a day, and others may only make 200. If you are a 500 widget-a-day maker, it may frustrate you to have a 200 widget-a-day maker reporting to you. You may be able to motivate that person to make 300 a day at some point, but they may never be capable of making 500. It's important to meet people where they are, for your own sanity and for your direct report's confidence. We have to understand a person's capabilities in order to help them maintain an appropriate workload and keep them accountable to it.

As employees learn their jobs, they will become faster and more efficient over time and should be able to take on more. We have to embrace, however, that they may still have a workload ceiling that is less than we'd like. Unfortunately, there is no way to test for this before hiring someone. This is something to monitor over time, though, because we may be able to delegate more and expect new levels of accountability as they grow into their role.

In addition to delegating appropriately, another way to keep people accountable is to have written policies that you go over on day one of employment. These policies should be in an employee handbook (even if that's just a stapled packet of papers), and employees should sign a document saying the policies have been explained to them and questions about them have been answered. Managers frequently have problems when they try to keep people accountable to "unwritten rules" at the office. The solution is to write them down. An employee can't argue with written policies that have been reviewed and agreed to by the employee via their signature.

Regular feedback with specific praise along the way can also help with accountability. Even if you only have formal evaluations annually, you can still have informal reviews quarterly (or even monthly) to check in with your direct report on progress toward work goals. If your employees know they must be prepared for these conversations with a progress report, they are much more likely to make headway on their goals.

Some managers resent that they need to praise people for just doing their job. "Years ago, you just did what you were told, and your paycheck was how you were appreciated," is a phrase I've heard many times. Younger generations respond better to specific praise, and if this is a method for keeping them happy and motivated, they will do a better job for you.

As I mentioned it Chapter Four, it can be helpful to think about what, specifically, you like about what they did and then compliment that specific behavior. For example, "I really liked the agenda you prepared for the meeting. Having time allotments for each agenda item really kept us on track." If there are multiple things you liked, choose the one you'd like to see again in the future. If an employee just focuses on doing their job, you can praise hard work. "I really appreciate your staying late to finish up that project last night. That helps us stay on schedule, and our client will be so appreciative."

One of the most helpful things I learned from working closely with our company's president, Steve Anderson, is that if a subordinate makes a misstep, it's best to address it quickly, with clarity and honesty. When Steve finds himself frustrated or confused by someone's transgression, he often talks with the person that same day. I will say here that giving constructive feedback when you are very upset is not a good idea. If it takes you time to calm down, certainly take the time you need to ensure you are composed for the conversation. In the past, I would generally put off confronting the person altogether, telling myself it was surely an isolated incident and would not happen again. After it happened a few more times I would finally (begrudgingly) address it, and usually the person would be confused and upset that I didn't talk with them sooner.

When we allow people to repeatedly do things that hurt or frustrate us, we are essentially teaching them that the behavior is acceptable to us. By not saying anything is wrong, we are consenting to their behavior. When we finally address the fact that we're not okay with the behavior, the person doing it can feel betrayed. Just when they learned what we have taught (that the behavior is acceptable), it feels as though the rules have suddenly been changed.

It can be challenging to manage direct reports who are not meeting your expectations or not meeting deadlines. To keep them accountable, I typically have a conversation up front to ensure they understand what I need them to do by when. If I am building trust, I will usually check in with the person about halfway to the deadline, to see how it's coming along. If they tell me they have an outline or a draft, I will ask to see it. If they hesitate (because they haven't done anything yet), they typically won't say so. Instead, they may say, "I have to put a few more finishing touches on it before I share it." I try to nail down a date when the draft might be ready for me to see in the next day or so, and then even if they have to scramble to get the document together, it's a catalyst for them to work on it.

If the deadline arrives and your direct report doesn't have the task done, don't just let them off the hook by saying, "Oh, it's okay. I know you're really busy." (the passive approach) and don't criticize them by saying, "You're really gonna make our department look bad!" (the aggressive approach). You can address them using the assertive conversation model I introduced in my first book *Shut Up and Lead*:

Step One: Describe the behavior. ("I have noticed...")

Step Two: Explain how it makes you feel. ("When this happens, I feel/am [one word].")

Step Three: Explain the changes you would like to see. ("I would ask/prefer...")

Using this example, you might say (using conversational words):

1. I've noticed the research for this project is not finished.

2. I'm concerned. We need the research findings before I can take the next step, so this puts the project behind schedule.

3. In the future, I'd prefer to know a few days in advance if you think you won't be able to meet a deadline, so I can make alternate plans. But for now, I'd like to have the research in hand in the next day or two. Can you get it to me by Friday?

When we're managing a relationship with a peer and following similar steps to keep them accountable, the challenge is that we don't have authority over them. We need leverage if they are consistently missing deadlines. Many people will go directly to the peer's supervisor to complain. This is a misstep politically and can also harm the working relationship with your peer. If deadlines continue to be missed, you can have an assertive conversation with your peer:

1. I've noticed that you're having difficulty meeting deadlines on this project, and although we've talked about it many times, and you've promised it would improve, it's not getting any better.

2. I'm worried that this project is falling behind, and I'm concerned our group's lack of progress will affect other company goals.

3. My next step is to talk with your supervisor to see how we can work through this. I'd like you to be part of that conversation. When are you available for us to meet with her?

With this conversation, you're telling your peer that it's not okay with you that they miss deadlines, and you intend to take action to try to solve the problem. By inviting your peer to come with you to discuss it with their supervisor, you're letting them know that you would say nothing to their supervisor that you wouldn't feel comfortable saying in front of them. This tells your peer that you are authentic and honest and truly want to solve the problem, not maliciously get them in trouble.

If we presume that people come to work wanting to do a good job, there are many legitimate reasons someone may have trouble meeting deadlines: the deadlines are unrealistic, the person's workload may be too heavy, the person committed to help you without realizing the time involved, or the person was "voluntold" to help and not consulted about their time/ability to do the work.

Some of my CEO clients become frustrated by a perceived lack of urgency in their companies, when employees are not working quickly and efficiently on a consistent basis. John Kotter, in his book *A Sense of Urgency*, tells us that leaders need to role model true urgency. "Behaving urgently," he writes, "does not mean constantly running around, screaming 'faster faster,' creating too much stress for others, and then becoming frustrated when no one else completes every goal tomorrow." He calls that false urgency. He goes on to explain that true urgency requires patience and a realistic view of how long reaching goals takes. If we, as role models, come to work every day with determination to make progress toward goal achievement, and role model the persistent action toward that end, we will be behaving with true urgency.[22]

It's important to not make negative assumptions. With that as a foundation, your tone of voice, your body language, and the words you choose when having assertive conversations will be delivered in a curious, problem-solving light instead of an annoyed, criticizing manner. Healthy workplace relationships require us to work with people who are not like us to solve problems and achieve company goals. When someone behaves in ways we would not, it doesn't mean they are wrong or incompetent or have ulterior motives; it just means that they are different than us.

We are always faced with the choice to presume good intent or ill intent with those we encounter. If we choose to believe people have good intent, we are inviting trust and also taking a risk. We may get burned. But the upside of having a solid relationship is so great that I think it's worthwhile to take the chance nearly every time. Even if the person turns out to be ill-intentioned, you've proceeded in accordance with your values and have done your best to give the relationship a decent chance of succeeding.

Pro Tip from Katlynn Henry, Senior Learning & Development Specialist at State Auto Insurance

It's truly rewarding, as a leader, to be able to meet your employee where they are; and as an employee to know you're being heard and recognized - it builds and reinforces trust. Each week, have your employee document in a quick email or shared document their top three successes of the prior week, three things they are focused on this week, and where you can help them. The successes ensure you are recognizing what is important to them; areas of focus provide insight, timeline, and accountability; and where you can help provides a lifeline. All open the lines of communication and nurture trust.

Chapter Seven – Key Points

- Give direct reports small, manageable tasks they can do with little guidance. As they handle these successfully, challenge them with progressively more difficult tasks.

- Establish an employee's ideal workload so that you have a benchmark against which to hold them accountable.

- People have different workload capacities. It's important to understand a person's capabilities in order to delegate to them appropriately, help them maintain an appropriate workload, and keep them accountable to assignments. They will become more proficient at their jobs over time.

- Don't try to keep people accountable to "unwritten rules" at the office. Create an employee handbook that outlines your expectations. Ask employees to sign a document saying the policies have been explained to them and questions about them have been answered.

- Regular feedback with specific praise along the way helps with accountability. If your employees are happy, they will be motivated to do a better job.

- If an employee does something that frustrates or confuses you, address it quickly with clarity and honesty.

- When we allow people to repeatedly do things that hurt or frustrate us, we are teaching them that the behavior is acceptable to us.

- To keep others accountable, have a conversation up front to ensure they understand what you need them to do by when.

- If a direct report is not meeting your expectations, have an assertive conversation:

  o Step One: Describe the behavior. ("I have noticed...")

  o Step Two: Explain how it makes you feel. ("When this happens, I feel/am [one word].")

  o Step Three: Explain the changes you would like to see. ("I would ask/prefer...")

- If a peer is not meeting your expectations, begin with an assertive conversation. If the behavior continues, invite your peer to join you in meeting with his or her supervisor to discuss potential solutions.

- Managers can role model urgency by coming to work every day with determination to make progress toward goal achievement and taking persistent action toward that end.

- When someone behaves in ways we would not, it doesn't mean they are wrong or incompetent or have ulterior motives; it just means that they are different than us.

Foster Trust and Set Boundaries

P eople always talk about "earning" someone's trust. I don't like to think about it this way, because it assumes that people are not to be trusted, so we must prove ourselves first. It's like being guilty until proven innocent. There is a wonderful book called *Trustology* by Richard Fagerlin in which the author suggests that giving trust as a default comes from presuming good intent in others. When trust is violated, giving the person a chance to explain their actions without operating on a negative assumption about what they did will keep trust in the relationship.[23]

When someone steps on our toes, many of us assume the worst and avoid that person for a few days while we marinate in our anger. Avoidance is a lose-lose conflict management strategy, and it doesn't move the relationship forward. When someone is actively avoiding me, which may just mean they are not speaking to me, I assume they don't feel safe enough to be honest with me. I try to make it clear to them that disagreeing with me is welcome and that it will help our relationship if I understand more about why they feel the way they do. Conflict in relationships can often be instructive and helpful, if it's handled properly. Conflict is only a problem when it leads to more conflict.

As I mentioned earlier, I spent most of my adult life being a people-pleaser. When someone upset me, I rationalized the hurt by telling myself it wasn't important. I did that so I would not have to confront the person who hurt me. This took me a very long time to figure out. I have been practicing assertiveness for some time now, and I find that being vulnerable and forthcoming with how I feel, though scary, leads to richer relationships. When someone violates my trust, I just address it. Nobody gets out of bed every morning with a plan to upset me. If I let go of negative assumptions and approach the person who hurt me with curiosity about how they perceived what happened, I usually get a satisfying answer that doesn't damage the relationship.

Some people are just plain mean or unreasonable. Often, their behavior has nothing to do with you. It's from years of faulty programing and negative self-talk. As children, we don't get to choose the people in our lives, so some of us grew up with bad role models who have damaged how we think about ourselves, others, and the world. We do have the power to decide, as adults, who we want to keep in our lives, how we talk to ourselves about ourselves and others, and how we behave in the world. We choose who we are every day, in every moment, with every word we say and every thing we do. As an executive coach, I have seen firsthand how dramatically people change when they decide they want to become a better version of themselves, are motivated to do what it takes to get there, and are working with a coach or some other accountability partner.

Trust is definitely a risk. There are times when there are enough red flags popping up in our head to warrant mistrust. If we decide to not trust, we are safe, but we forfeit the potential positive outcomes. Mistrust is comfortable. We need not wonder what will happen. We need not engage. We stay in our cocoon.

In the management roles I've held, I've often chosen to trust. I have gotten burned occasionally, but I would still choose it again in each case. The courage it takes to be vulnerable and trust others has led me to amazing relationships, happiness, goal fulfillment, and confidence. When I get knocked down by someone I trusted, I've seen myself rise again, and that has been profoundly instructional. We learn so much from adversity. We may not seek it out, but when it finds us, we will grow.

Although trust can be a wonderful conduit to connection, sometimes we simply must set boundaries.

I saw an unattributed Facebook post that said, "People who get mad when you set boundaries in your life are likely the ones who were benefiting from your lack of boundaries to begin with." That resonated with me. As I said earlier, I spent most of my adult life being very passive. My boundaries were often violated, and I would allow it to happen. Once I started to set boundaries and stick to them, some people got mad. I now imagine that when this happens, that person was likely taking advantage of me. When I see them get mad, and understand why that may be, I feel much better about sticking up for myself.

Boundaries allow us to decide which behaviors are acceptable in our lives and which are not. Boundaries protect us from being hurt. Some people routinely cross boundaries. Examples include people who are verbally or emotionally abusive, are controlling, have an addiction, or are selfish. When my boundaries were violated, I often wondered if I was overreacting or being overly sensitive. This thought came to mind because I was looking for a reason to give in to keep the peace. I didn't want anyone to be mad at me, so I tried to rationalize my passive behavior by telling myself that I was the person with the problem, not them. My advice to others in light of what I've learned is don't make yourself small, compliant, or quiet. You have a right to decide what you will and will not do, and holding true to your feelings and values will help stave off the resentment you would otherwise feel if you complied with something distasteful.

We teach people how to treat us, and we get what we tolerate. Setting a boundary is an idle threat unless we keep people accountable to it. We have to love and respect ourselves enough not only to set boundaries, but also to keep them. Our time and energy are finite and precious; only we get to decide how to spend them.

One boundary that poses a frequent challenge is navigating relationships at work that have spilled over into personal friendships. I have had clients who are close friends with a peer at work and then one of them is promoted to become the other person's supervisor. The promoted person still wants to hunt and fish on the weekends with his friend, but now keeping that friend accountable at work becomes tough. One client I coached who had a personal relationship with a co-worker came in one morning to hear the friend talking about the activities they shared over the weekend and joking about a personal item my client had shared. A line was crossed, and it was enough for my client to swear off ever spending time on a weekend with a co-worker again.

Sometimes it's not either party, but rather others in the organization who are uncomfortable with the relationship continuing. The assumption of favoritism may undermine a supervisor/subordinate relationship before an unfair incident ever actually occurs.

Gallup, an American analytics and advisory company, has long touted the importance of having a best friend at work. Their research, described in a *Business Journal* article, shows a concrete link between having a best friend at work and the effort employees expend in their job.[24] For example, women who strongly agree they have a best friend at work are 63% likely to be engaged workers, while only 29% of women are engaged when they say they don't agree with that statement. Gallup also found those with a best friend at work are better at engaging customers, produce higher quality work, have higher well-being, and are less likely to get injured on the job. LinkedIn also studied the benefits of having a best friend at work. They found that especially with staff ages 18-24, having a best friend at work improves their happiness, motivation, and productivity.[25]

I believe there is no "right" way to handle all workplace relationships. It greatly depends on the type of personal relationship that exists. Often, a heart-to-heart conversation where boundaries are discussed is enough to set expectations that will allow the relationship to continue both at work and outside of work. If one person expects exceptional treatment from their friend at work, the boundary (discussion of fairness and impartiality) must be set and adhered to in order to ensure a comfortable continuation of the dual relationship.

Pro Tip from Gary Baker, Director of Marketing & Public Relations at The Energy Cooperative

Developing trust within a management team can only be achieved by creating a culture of honesty and loyalty. Trust can be embedded in the team by sharing high level management discussions that are not confidential, fairly common and on the record. Conversations by the senior management team when shared with managers, supervisors and others create a sense of belonging and ownership.

Keeping the team close to the decision making and "in the loop" will bond the team. On the same note, when confidentiality within the senior management team is in place, it must be observed. That commitment exhibits a culture and sets the example of trust.

Chapter Eight – Key Points

- When trust is violated, give the person a chance to explain their actions without operating on a negative assumption about what they did to keep trust in the relationship.

- Avoidance is a lose-lose conflict management strategy, and it doesn't move the relationship forward. Conflict in relationships can be helpful, when handled properly.

- Some people are mean or unreasonable from years of faulty programing and negative self-talk. Their behavior often has nothing to do with you.

- We choose who we are every day, in every moment, with every word we say and every thing we do.

- Boundaries allow us to decide which behaviors are acceptable in our lives and which are not.

- Work relationships that spill over into friendships outside work sometimes result in the assumption of favoritism by others at work that may undermine a supervisor/subordinate relationship before an unfair incident ever occurs.

- Research studies by both Gallup and LinkedIn show that having a best friend at work leads to greater happiness and engagement. Set boundaries and discuss clear expectations to ensure business relationships are not compromised by a personal friendship.

CHAPTER NINE

Motivation and Delegation

How to motivate others seems to elude many managers and leaders I've coached. Each generation differs from the one that came before, but there are approaches that work to motivate most people, which we will cover in this chapter.

What do employees want? My client, anesthesiologist Dr. William Kelley with the Ohio State University Wexner Medical Center, mentioned in a presentation that he believes professionals want three things: transparency, equity, and cash.[26] Although we will discuss all three in this chapter, I could not agree with him more about the need for transparency. The leadership teams I've worked with learn this early in the consulting process, because employees often tell me managers don't communicate sufficiently, and employees often cannot articulate a manager's vision or even current departmental goals. Many executives are simply not transparent or vulnerable with one another in the workplace. When we deeply understand ourselves and others and are willing to share our thoughts and feelings at work, we become much more productive and efficient.

In his book *The Speed of Trust*, Steven M.R. Covey says that transparency is "based on the *principles* of honesty, openness, integrity, and authenticity" and "is gaining recognition as a critical value in high-trust organizations." He writes that being transparent "gives (people) a sense of comfort and confidence because they know there's nothing being hidden." The premise of the book is that when we trust others, we can get things done quickly.[27] Discussions I've had with clients in coaching over the years has led to my corroboration that if people are comfortable, confident, and not worrying about hidden agendas and hoarding of information, they can focus more at work and, thus, accomplish tasks faster.

Dr. Kelly articulated that, to him, equity is the belief that if you work hard, you get more. When I worked in state government, I experienced firsthand how difficult it was to work in an inequitable environment. I lasted two years there and then sought a workplace in which my hard work was acknowledged with more pay or flexibility. In his speech, Dr. Kelly included in his definition of equity that professionals want to work in an environment where there is no playing favorites, no top-secret ways to behave appropriately, and no destructive competition.[28]

The third thing professionals typically want, Dr. Kelly said, is cash (take-home pay). He said, "If you don't have the first two (transparency and equity), the only thing they care about is money. If you're re-negotiating a contract or promoting someone or hiring, and all the candidate talks about is cash, don't hire or promote them, because there's a good chance they will leave for more money."[29] How often have we heard employees complain about not being paid enough? If we pay people well, salary becomes a non-issue.

Journalist and digital consultant John Boitnott wrote an article for Inc.com[30] about why we should pay employees above average wages:

- We will attract more A-players which will help with our bottom line

- Above average salaries generate an expectation of above average work

- Word-of-mouth recruiting may improve (if we also engage them through praise and attention)

- Employees will stay longer, so we'll keep their knowledge and growing productivity in-house

- It takes away financial anxiety at home so they can focus more on work

- They will be fairly rewarded, which is just right

- With top-notch employees, you'll need less of them to do the work

Once salary is a non-issue, we can focus on other ways to motivate employees. In his book *Drive: The Surprising Truth About What Motivates Us*, Daniel Pink introduces research findings that show that people enjoy solving problems, but when external rewards are introduced, people are less motivated and less productive. Pink writes, "Most businesses haven't caught up to this new understanding of what motivates us. They continue to pursue practices such as short-term incentive plans and pay-for-performance schemes in the face of mounting evidence that such measures usually don't work and often do harm."[31] By offering a reward, managers are alerting employees that the task is undesirable.

There are many easy, low-cost methods to motivate employees:

Career Coaching:

- Discuss their career path and ask questions about where they see themselves in the future. Don't be content with the answer, "I'm happy to do whatever the company needs me to do." What do *they* want to do?

- Challenge them to explain how they might best use their strengths for the good of the company.

- Create more promotional layers and explain the expectations of each one, so they understand what to improve in order to move up.

- Set short-term goals and meet frequently to discuss progress.

- Ask questions to help them understand the culture and office politics.

- Develop a mentoring program.

Provide Learning/Training Opportunities:

- Provide tuition reimbursement or invest in their training.

- Put them in charge of a charitable event.

- Offer job shadowing.

- Have brown bag lunches where different departments share information.

- Share articles, books, and information with them.

- Have them track their own progress and share their measurements with you.

- Invest in an executive coach.

Allow for Creativity/Flexibility:

- Let them figure things out and do it their own way; let them take calculated risks.

- Give them a variety of projects, so they may uncover and utilize their strengths.

- Let them work in teams and with higher ups when appropriate.

- Ask them what motivates them and implement what you can.

Delegation, the act of assigning a task to another person, is also a way to motivate others. When considering what to delegate, don't think about giving away what you least want to do. Instead, think about who has the information needed or the expertise to complete the task. If nobody else has the information or expertise, decide if the task provides an opportunity for someone to learn a new skill. Could they add it to their job description or resume? Would they be excited to learn it? Tasks that recur and can be taught to anyone are ripe for delegation.

Delegation does not mean just dropping a task on someone's desk. Usually it involves some instruction. We often think we don't have time to delegate. We could do the task ourselves by the time we explain it to someone else, right? I hear this frequently. If we explain it once and the task recurs, the time it takes to explain it once saves many hours of doing the task in the future. Once again, it's helpful to look at the instruction time as time saved later.

When delegating, I recommend giving away anything that doesn't take your specific brain to do. There is a reason you hold the position you do. Your unique strengths are being leveraged for the good of the company. As a company leader, it's important that you spend time doing the things only someone at your level can do.

That said, this is a self-imposed rule with which I struggle frequently. One Thursday night, I found myself at the office at 7 p.m. making copies. I was already late leaving the office, but here I was doing a task that didn't take my specific brain. As I realized this, I asked myself why I was doing it. I realized that the person who would do this for me would not be in the next day, and I was too impatient to wait for Monday. The fact was that I didn't need it before Monday. My impatience was driving me to stay late to do work that didn't have to be done at that moment, nor by me.

Observe yourself to not only catch yourself behaving in ways that are unhelpful, but to reflect on what benefit you're receiving from the activity. We don't do anything without a payoff. I'm a recovering perfectionist, so my payoff is usually doing it the way I want, when I want. I struggle with patience, so it's a payoff when I don't have to wait for others. The problem is that I'm wasting time with an activity I should delegate, and I am missing the larger payoff of doing more important and productive tasks with that time – like spending it with family in this example.

Pro Tip from Claudia Pankowski, Director of Regulatory Compliance at Buckeye Partners

Motivating others does not happen by simply role modeling hard work. People have to know that we care about them. I have been challenged in the past with perfectionism, and it negatively affected me and those I supervised. We don't have to work harder and be more demanding of others to be successful. I've learned, instead, that we have to listen well so those we supervise feel valued. We have to say no more, so our workload allows time to truly manage people. We have to take time to meet with those we supervise to learn what motivates them and what talents they possess, so we might delegate appropriately. We must teach and lift up others so they are confident contributors to the company's success.

Chapter Nine – Key Points

- Management transparency leads to motivation and trust.

- Being rewarded for the work you do (equity) is motivational for many employees.

- If we pay people above-averages wages, salary becomes a non-issue.

- Short-term incentive plans and pay-for-performance programs usually don't work and often do harm.

- There are many low-cost ways to motivate employees:
  - Career Coaching
  - Provide Learning/Training Opportunities
  - Allow for Creativity/Flexibility

- When considering what to delegate, don't think about giving away what you least want to do. Instead, choose someone who has the information needed or the expertise to complete the task.

- Delegation involves instruction, and people sometimes resent having to take time to train others. Explaining something once or twice to someone often far outweighs the time you would spend repeatedly completing the task yourself into the future.

CHAPTER TEN

Empowerment

M ost of us would say we want to empower our direct reports, and I have found that few of us actually do. Let's start with what empower means: to give someone the authority or power to do something; to make someone stronger and more confident, especially in controlling their life and claiming their rights.[32] It's about giving employees the latitude to use their creativity to solve problems independently, without having to get approval from higher ups.

Here are some ways we can truly empower others:

Value Others. A basic need of all people is to feel valued. Empowerment starts with caring about others, so they can be confident in their abilities and happy to work with us. Show you care by expressing appreciation regularly. Use the words please and thank you when interacting with others. I'm amazed at how frequently I hear the complaint that people in the workplace are not using these two simple words that can convey respect and gratitude.

Validate People. To validate someone, recognize, acknowledge and accept how someone is feeling. You can validate people even when you disagree with them. We often think we are helping when someone expresses a negative emotion and we respond with something positive. If someone says, "I'm so frustrated that my presentation went so poorly," when it clearly did not go well, and we say, "It was fine. You were great!" then we are not validating them. It's validating to say, "Yes, I saw that you were struggling a bit. I can understand how you would be frustrated when you worked so hard to prepare. What do you think threw you off?"

Delegate Appropriately. This can be scary for all of you driven perfectionists out there, but it's a necessary component of great management and leadership. You should only be doing what takes your specific brain. Anything that can be taught to someone else, especially repetitive tasks that are weekly or monthly, should be delegated. If you hoard work because you are a perfectionist, I guarantee you are wasting time and not living up to your leadership potential.

Allow Autonomy. Micromanagement (controlling every aspect of the work delegated) kills motivation and breeds mistrust. Ask yourself if you have confidence in your ability to train others and if you are modeling the behaviors you want to see in your team members. If the answer is yes, then you should feel comfortable letting direct reports operate with less oversight. If you don't have that confidence because you haven't fully put your trust in your team, then it's time to consider steps you can take to train them better and build that trust.

Permit Mistakes. If we give people authority and autonomy, they will make mistakes. Making mistakes is how we learn and grow. I bet you can remember a big mistake you made that you felt viscerally. When it happened, you thought, "I will never, ever, EVER do that again." Those lessons are far more poignant than someone simply telling you it's a bad idea or swooping in to save you with a solution of their own. We learn best when we feel the pain of failure and subsequently have to solve a tough problem. If we never failed, we'd never be able to make tough decisions independently. Failure is part of gaining experience and resilience. It's a disservice to our subordinates if we solve all of their problems.

Coach; Don't Tell. A feeling of empowerment results when someone has figured a problem out for themselves. Don't just tell your direct reports the answers; coach them to find the solution themselves. It builds confidence and allows them to become better problem solvers. Coaching is about asking questions to help people think things through. Ask questions to lead the person to the answer you already know.

Foster Healthy Team Dynamics. Several years ago, Google focused on building the perfect team. They called the initiative Project Aristotle[33], and they studied hundreds of Google's teams to figure out why some were more successful than others. After observing over 100 groups for more than a year, they concluded that effective teams felt psychological safety - the belief that the team is safe for interpersonal risk-taking and its members are certain they won't be embarrassed, rejected, or punished for speaking up. They discovered that psychological safety was made up of two key elements: 1) allowing all members equal amounts of sharing ideas and listening and 2) being able to read non-verbal cues and have emotional conversations.

If we strive to build a learning culture by practicing these methods of empowerment, we will teach employees that celebrating our successes is just as important as learning from our failures. Empowering employees lifts morale and creates a safe environment in which to grow.

Pro Tip from Dr. Naci Bozkir, Ophthalmologist at Holzer Clinic

Perfection is something I've struggled with through the years, demanding it of both myself and others. Although perfectionists often have higher levels of motivation and conscientiousness, there are downsides. Many perfectionists are overly self-critical and frequently disappointed in others, resulting in unnecessary suffering. Perfection has no place in empowering others. I've read about a concept called excellentism, where one strives for excellence, not perfection. If we endeavor to be excellent, we allow space for mistakes. Mistakes are how we learn, so it's important for our own well-being and for those we manage to accept mistakes as part of our growth as we learn to become better managers and empower others.

Chapter Ten – Key Points

- Empowerment is about giving someone the authority to solve problems independently, without having to get approval from higher ups.

- A basic need of all people is to feel valued, so empowerment starts with caring about others.

- It's important to validate others, which means we recognize, acknowledge and accept how someone is feeling.

- Only do what takes your specific brain. Anything that can be taught to someone else, especially repetitive tasks that are weekly or monthly, should be delegated.

- If you have confidence in your ability to train others and if you are modeling the behaviors you want to see in your team members, then you should feel comfortable letting direct reports operate with little oversight.

- We learn best when we feel the pain of failure and subsequently have to solve a tough problem.

- If we coach direct reports to find the solution themselves, instead of just telling them the answers, it builds confidence and allows them to become better problem solvers.

- Research from Google concluded that the most effective teams feel psychological safety - the belief that the team is safe for interpersonal risk-taking and its members won't be embarrassed, rejected, or punished for speaking up.

Section Three: Review and Restructure

"Great leaders inspire people
to have confidence in themselves."

- Eleanor Roosevelt

CHAPTER ELEVEN

Evaluation

I continue to be surprised by companies who haven't evaluated employees in several years. I've heard many different reasons: they expect a raise every time and we can't or don't give them one, I'm terrible at giving constructive feedback, everyone's doing well so we don't need to tell them that, they don't react well to feedback, we don't have time. Although I've been in the workforce for over 30 years, I continue to appreciate someone helping me understand how I'm perceived by others and how I might improve. We can all learn and grow, but we can't do it without honest feedback.

Having formal annual reviews supplemented by informal, quarterly check-ins is a good way to keep people accountable throughout the year, which also provides a forum for you to discuss anything of concern. One of my past employers asked us to set measurable, yearly goals and then split them up into smaller, quarterly action steps to support the overall goals. I was very motivated because I created the goals myself. My supervisor would meet with me quarterly to assess progress, and I'm certain I was more productive because I would be held accountable to the action steps I created. Having these check-ins to discuss goals also shows employees they are valued and that you want them to succeed. I think it's also useful to have employee goals align with departmental goals and company goals. This alignment helps employees understand how their contributions support the overall strategic plan of the company.

Many supervisors who conduct regular evaluations overrate their employees. It's a sad reality that people fear giving honest, direct feedback. Sometimes it's because the person receiving the evaluation reacts in ways that make the evaluator uncomfortable, and the evaluator is unsure how to handle these reactions. Managers I've worked with have told me that they don't give honest reviews because the employee might cry, yell, or argue with them. This only tells me that we have to continue to practice assertive conversations so that we will learn how to better deal with those reactions.

I have found that poor reactions can be a subconscious method of protection. If I cry or yell every time I get honest feedback, then people will stop giving me feedback and I won't be hurt. If we can empathize with the person reacting while continuing to give feedback, everyone wins. A manager might say, "I see that this feedback is very upsetting to you. It's upsetting to me too, just in a different way. I really want you to succeed and this behavior is keeping you from your full potential. I'm confident we can come up with a solution together."

I have had coaching clients tell me they don't think reviews are fair. Some think their manager dislikes them and can't be impartial. It may be that they perceive the manager has a favorite employee and nobody else compares. The employee may think he or she is performing better than the manager thinks because the manager has unrealistic expectations. One remedy is to have others weigh in on the evaluation. One of my client companies does what I call a mini-360 before review time. In addition to the supervisor, the boss's boss, peers and direct reports also provide feedback. Comments are shared anonymously during the evaluation, and often the employee being reviewed leaves with a clear, impartial picture of how they are progressing.

Some managers simply don't see the usefulness in having a sit-down evaluation with a great employee. I think avoiding this meeting because you feel there is nothing to say is a big mistake. I find that the most motivated people are also those who strive to continuously learn and grow. They want to be held accountable. They want to feel valued. Prepare for these meetings as thoroughly as you do for the evaluations with the employees who are struggling on your team. Think about how you will challenge your great employees. Take notes during the meeting, so they see you plan to take action based on the conversation.

It's a wise idea to give employees a copy of the form that will be used to evaluate them on the first day of employment as part of their employee manual or policy guide. This way you can answer any questions they may have about how they will be rated and what consequences or rewards come from an especially good or especially poor evaluation right at the start. It's an effective way to communicate the behavioral expectations directly and honestly so there are no surprises later.

At Integrated Leadership Systems, we evaluate people not only on job-specific tasks, but also on their adherence to our stated company values, such as putting our team first, being trustworthy, being reliable, etc. Including your company values on an evaluation form tells your employees that you value both competence and character in your employees, which we know from *The Speed of Trust*, is the formula for creating trust. In a high-trust culture, your employees are more likely to get along with one another and less likely to leave.

Pro Tip from Kristina Eiting, General Manager Asphalt at Owens Corning

Be open to receiving constructive feedback about your own performance and be purposeful in your response. You will become more self-aware. Self-awareness opens the door to humility and objectivity. Objectivity removes emotion and opens the door to constructive connection.

Conduct constructive connections regularly. It is nearly impossible to create a trusting professional relationship without putting in the time. Provide examples of your own challenges and learnings. This lets your employees know you are human, that you are approachable, and it affords the opportunity for them to learn from your mistakes. Ensure feedback, objectives, and action items are clear and all ambiguity is removed. We all deserve to know what is expected of us. In all of the above, and all that you do as a leader, be genuine. Be yourself, your best self, for yourself and for your team.

Chapter Eleven - Key Points

- Having formal annual reviews supplemented by informal, quarterly check-ins is a good way to keep people accountable throughout the year.

- Continue to practice assertive conversations to learn how to better deal with poor reactions employees may have to honest feedback at their evaluations.

- In addition to the supervisor's feedback, you may consider having a mini-360 where the boss's boss, peers and direct reports also provide feedback. Comments may be shared anonymously during the evaluation, so the employee leaves with a clear, impartial picture of how they are progressing.

- Don't avoid evaluating your great employees. Prepare for these meetings as thoroughly as you do for those who are struggling on your team.

- Give employees a copy of their evaluation form on the first day of employment so you may answer questions they may have about how they will be rated and what consequences or rewards come from an especially good or especially poor evaluation.

- Including your company values on an evaluation form tells your employees that you value character as much as competence.

CHAPTER TWELVE

Termination

M ost managers are reluctant to fire employees. Often, managers tell me they feel guilty because they are causing a person to lose income which helps support a family. If you have communicated openly along the way about the unacceptable behavior and have provided an opportunity for the person to improve and succeed, then this failure is not yours. The employee has caused their own termination.

Communicating at the first sign of unwelcome behavior is critical. Some people are let go without explanation. This is a disservice not only to that person, but to future employers who may have to address the same behavior. Below is a process you may want to follow to evaluate and coach people before letting them go.

1. When you point out what needs to be changed, be specific about what you *do* want to see. Choose behavior that's obvious - you can clearly see it or not.

2. Choose a period of time in which they are expected to show improvement, so you can evaluate them at that time, and commit to coaching them along the way.

3. When you see the new behavior, call it out, praise them, and thank them for making an effort.

4. If you see the unwelcome behavior again, pull the person aside to address it right away.

5. If poor behavior continues, formalize the process with a Performance Improvement Plan (PIP) that outlines what behavioral changes you expect and the consequences (usually firing) if changes are not seen.

I encourage you to think about managing the emotional aspects of this process of improvement, as well as the behavioral. Many people assume that when they are given a PIP, they will be fired. If the employee views the situation as hopeless, they will simply give up with the assumption that nothing they do will be good enough to keep their job. To foster improvement and help the employee succeed, express confidence that they can turn this around.

If a manager strongly dislikes a subordinate, or the relationship is very strained, moving that subordinate (if practical) to another manager may help remedy the situation. I have seen cases where an employee is under a PIP when their manager leaves or there is a reorganization, and the employee is assigned a new manager who must take over the administration of the PIP. Sometimes the new manager is perplexed by the PIP and sees nothing overtly worrisome about the employee. Different managers have different expectations, so considering relationship aspects may also be worthwhile. A new manager may be better able to give hope to the employee.

Pro Tip from Claudia S. Herrington, Esq. CCEP, Senior Director of Compliance at JobsOhio & Adjunct Professor at Otterbein University

Terminating an employee is the most undesirable job responsibility I have had as a manager and leader in my career. It impacts the terminated individual's self-esteem and financial security. It affects company morale when employees, especially those who worked closely with the terminated employee, learn of a termination and have little-to-no factual understanding as to why an organization made the decision it did.

When poor performance or behavior occurs, I provide immediate and specific feedback to an employee on what, I hope, is an isolated incident. In the event of a subsequent incident, I still provide feedback, but I document the occurrence in real time so my recall is thorough and crisp. I believe patterns of behavior are telling. If I am concerned about the employee's poor performance or behavior, I avail myself to the appropriate corporate partners early to ensure the organization is protected from increased risk in the event of termination.

In the event of termination, I am direct and unapologetic, but gracious in what is always an uncomfortable final conversation with that employee. I give the employee time to process what I am saying in case there are next steps such as packing up an office, a change in benefits or the need to return corporate assets. At the end of the day, if an employee is not the right fit for the organization, termination is the right outcome for the employee so he or she can find another opportunity. Further, despite the sizeable upfront investment each organization makes in an employee, it is the right outcome for the organization as well.

Chapter Twelve - Key Points

- If you have communicated openly with an employee about unacceptable behavior and have provided an opportunity for the person to improve and succeed, then there is no need to feel guilty if you choose to fire them.

- Follow a process to evaluate and coach employees before letting them go:
  - Be specific about your behavioral expectations.
  - Choose a date by which you expect improvement.
  - Praise them if you see their behavior improve.
  - Correct unwelcome behavior if it happens again.
  - If poor behavior continues, formalize your expectations with a Performance Improvement Plan (PIP).

- Give employees hope and express confidence that they can improve following a PIP.

- If the working relationship between a supervisor and direct report is strained, consider reassigning the employee to a new manager who might have a different view of the behaviors displayed.

Conclusion

I hope this book has provided you with some practical ways to build relationships and engage others, as well as keep them accountable, so that you may practice effective management skills. Managing others is so rewarding, despite how difficult it can be along the way.

I hope you are encouraged by this book to start with yourself. We must first find ways to become better organized and put structures and processes in place to achieve our goals. Once we have that structure, we can then focus on encouraging others. There are so many things we can do to empower and praise others to help them achieve the purpose God intended for them. My hope is that this book has given you some options to consider for helping others achieve their dreams while you achieve yours. And finally, it's important to continue evaluating employees and helping some of them move on to other organizations if they are not a fit. It is a gift to help others find a workplace and occupation they love.

Do you remember an outstanding supervisor you've had in your career? Managers and leaders do what they do and rarely realize how much they've impacted the lives of others along the way. I have been blessed with some amazing supervisors throughout my career.

In addition to thinking of them with gratitude, I do what I can to emulate those people.

I will never forget an office manager with whom I worked at BellSouth Corporation in Washington, D.C. Her name is Marilyn Jordan, and she was by far the best communicator I had encountered to that point in my life. Just like those bracelets people used to wear that said WWJD (What Would Jesus Do), I often found myself in tough situations thinking What Would Marilyn Do? I valued her role modeling so much. In addition to her fantastic communication skills, she was very honest, direct, patient, and ethical. She made decisions in accordance with her values. As I continued to develop in my career, I never forgot Marilyn. In fact, I still strive to emulate her.

What a blessing we could be in this world if we could each choose one supervisor, like Marilyn, who we could hold onto as a lifelong role model in our minds, long after we lose physical contact. Engaging others by behaving as our best selves and helping others leverage their strengths for their own happiness and the betterment of their organization creates effective future supervisors for generations to come. I want this for my children and grandchildren. Don't you?

Management can be both challenging and rewarding. As difficult as it is to figure out how to best relate to each person you manage, the efficiency and productivity you can foster by taking time to do just that leads to tremendous business success. I wish you the patience to learn about others and practice new approaches until you find those that best work for you. I also wish you the courage to be vulnerable and imperfect and human.

Referenced Material

1 From an email exchange with Mark Henson, Chief Imagination Officer and founder of sparkspace, Columbus, OH.

2 Cohen, P. (2009, March 21-22). *The Naked Empress: Modern neuroscience and the concept of addiction.* Retrieved from https://seekhealing.org/downloads/Dr.Peter.Cohen.research-.The.naked.empress.pdf.

3 Suderman, J. (2015, December 17). *Is Leadership a Noun or Verb?* Retrieved from http://jeffsuderman.com/is-leadership-a-noun-or-a-verb.

4 House, R. & Hanges, P. & Ruiz-Quintanilla, S. & Dorfman, P. & Falkus, S. & Ashkanasy, N. (1999). Cultural influences on leadership and organizations: Project GLOBE. Advances in Global Leadership. 1.

5 House, R. & Hanges, Paul & Ruiz-Quintanilla, S. & Dorfman, Peter & Falkus, S. & Ashkanasy, Neal. (1999). Cultural influences on leadership and organizations: Project GLOBE. Advances in Global Leadership. 1.

6 Covey, S. R. (1989) *The 7 Habits of Highly Effective People: Powerful Lessons in Personal Change.* New York, NY: Free Press.

7 Levitin, D. (2014), *The Organized Mind: Thinking Straight in the Age of Information Overload.* New York, NY: Penguin Random House, p.16, 96.

8 Allen, D. (2001). *Getting Things Done: The Art of Stress-Free Productivity.* United Kingdom: Penguin Books.

9 Levitin, D. (2014), *The Organized Mind: Thinking Straight in the Age of Information Overload.* New York, NY: Penguin Random House, p. 68.

10 Allen, D. (2001). *Getting Things Done: The Art of Stress-Free Productivity.* United Kingdom: Penguin Books.

11 Doran, G. T. (1981). *There's a S.M.A.R.T. way to write management's goals and objectives.* Management Review (AMA FORUM) 70 (11): 35-36.

12 Covey, S. M.R. (2006). *The Speed of Trust: The One Thing That Changes Everything.* New York, NY: Free Press, p. 54.

13 Fatemi, F. (2018, September 28) *The True Cost Of A Bad Hire -- It's More Than You Think.* Retrieved from https://www. forbes. com/ sites/ falonfatemi/2016/09/28/ the-true-cost-of-a-bad-hire-its-more-than-you-think/ #3c8d94674aa4

14 Blanchard, K. & Johnson, S. (2003). *The One Minute Manager.* New York, NY: William Morrow.

15 Zak, P. (2013) *The Moral Molecule: How Trust Works.* New York, NY: Plume.

16 Monbiot, G. (2014, October 14) *The Age of Loneliness is Killing Us*. Retrieved from https://www. theguardian.com/ commentisfree/ 2014/oct/14/age-of-loneliness-killing-us.

17 Rath, T. & Conchie, B. (2009, March 26). *What Strong Teams Have in Common: The five sure signs of an excellent team*. Retrieved from https://news.gallup.com/businessjournal/113341/what-strong-teams-common.aspx.

18 McLeod, S. A. (2019, January 11). *Cognitive Behavioral Therapy*. Retrieved from https://www.simplypsychology.org/cognitive-therapy.html.

19 Shrestha, P. (2018, April 1). *Actor-Observer Bias*. Retrieved from https://www.psychestudy.com/social/actor-observer-bias.

20 Neo, S. (2019, July 22). *4 Types of Communication Challenges in Multicultural Organizations*. Retrieved from https://www.trainingindustry.com/blog/blog-entries/4-types-of-communication-challenges-in-multicultural-organizations.aspx.

21 Eagleman, D. (2015). *The Brain: The Story of You*. New York, NY: Pantheon Books, p. 33-34.

22 Based on the assertive communication suggestions offered by psychological researcher and clinician John Gottman.

23 Kotter, J. (2008). A Sense of Urgency. Boston, MA: Harvard Business Press, p. 117-118.

24 Fagerlin, R. (2013). Trustology: The Art and Science of Leading High-Trust Teams. Wise Guys Publishing LLC.

25 Rath, T. & Conchie, B. (2009, March 26). What Strong Teams Have in Common: The five sure signs of an excellent team. Retrieved from https://news.gallup.com/businessjournal/113341/what-strong-teams-common.aspx.

26 Zimmerman, K. (2015, December 5). Can Having A Best Friend At Work Make You More Productive? Retrieved from https://www.forbes.com/sites/kaytiezimmerman/2016/12/05/can-having-a-best-friend-at-work-make-you-more-productive/#64727d4b43bb.

27 Kelly, W. (2019, June 6). Integrated Leadership Systems Leadership Institute presentation.

28 Covey, S. M.R. (2006). The Speed of Trust: The One Thing That Changes Everything. New York, NY: Free Press, p. 154.

29 Kelly, W. (2019, June 6). Integrated Leadership Systems Leadership Institute presentation.

30 Kelly, W. (2019, June 6). Integrated Leadership Systems Leadership Institute presentation.

31 Boitnott, J. (2018, June 18). 7 Reasons You Should Pay Your Employees Above-Average Salaries. Retrieved from https://www.inc.com/john-boitnott/7-reasons-you-should-pay-your-employees-above-average-salaries.html.

32 Pink, D. (2011). Drive: The Surprising Truth About What Motivates Us. New York, NY: Riverhead Books.

33 Retrieved from https://www.merriam-webster.com/dictionary/empower.

34 Duhigg, C. (2016, February 25). What Google Learned From Its Quest to Build the Perfect Team. Retrieved from https://www.nytimes.com/2016/02/28/magazine/what-google-learned-from-its-quest-to-build-the-perfect-team.html.

Acknowledgments

I thank God for giving me the courage to use the gifts with which He blessed me. I know lots of people write books, but despite having a journalism degree, publishing has been an intimidating, humbling process for me.

My husband, Bob, and sons, Carson and Connor, have been wonderful supporters of mine. Thank you, my amazing family, for giving me comic relief and comfort when I need it. Through your love, I am constantly reminded of what's most important in life.

I can't possibly thank enough all the amazing clients I've been blessed to work with since I began my consulting career at Integrated Leadership Systems in 2006. It is because of your honesty and vulnerability that I have been able to gain insight to use in helping others through consulting, executive coaching, training and public speaking. Your willingness to share your stories have helped countless others, and I'm so grateful and humbled to facilitate that knowledge sharing.

There have been a handful of extremely talented leaders who have helped me better understand leadership and who have supported me as I continue to improve, and I thank these incredible role models from the bottom of my heart: Jim Negron of Corna Kokosing, Jim Matesich and Sarah Schwab of Matesich Distributing, Marissa Buckley of Security First Insurance, and Scott Thompson of Thompson Concrete.

Without Steve Anderson, president of Integrated Leadership Systems, welcoming me onto his staff, mentoring and coaching me, and giving me a chance to learn and grow and make mistakes, I would not have the amazing job and life I have today. Thanks, Steve, for all you've done to help me become a better businesswoman, leader, manager, mom, and friend. You are so inspirational, and I have enjoyed watching you change the world. In addition, I thank my amazing colleagues at ILS who have been collaborative, validating, empathetic and incredibly supportive: Jane Ahern, Charlisa Anderson, Tyler Armstrong, Dr. Rebecca Morrissey, Mario Rodriguez, Dr. Katie Sprague, and Dr. Lisa White. I love you all so much.

Some of my clients and professional associates who I hold in very high esteem have been instrumental in adding to this book by either offering a professional tip at the end of a chapter, reading my book in advance of publishing, or allowing me to include an example from an interaction I had with them. Thank you so much to these incredible people whom I admire immensely: Brian Ahearn, Karen Bailey, Gary Baker, Dr. Naci Bozkir, Pam Cummings, Kristina Eiting, Mary Garrick, Tammy Grimes, Katlynn Henry, Claudia Herrington,

Dr. William Kelly, John Palmer, Claudia Pankowski, Bill Patton, Donna Stevens, Mitch Vincent, and Owen Wyss.

Thank you to my very talented, bestselling author coaches, Scott Allan (https://scottallanauthor.com/) and Lise Cartwright (http://lisecartwright.com/). I appreciated their patience and advice so much. In addition to my skilled editor, Hannah Magnusson (https://www.greatgreyeditorial.com), I want to thank my son, Carson Clark, and my sister, Joyce Romanski, who gave this book a final proofread after I changed and added a thousand little things before publishing. I love and appreciate you both so much.

About the Author

M.J. Clark is the vice president of Integrated Leadership Systems (www.integratedleader.com), based in Ohio. She serves clients all over the country in numerous industries as a leadership consultant, executive coach and workplace trainer. She is the author of *Shut Up and Lead: A Communicator's Guide to Quiet Leadership* and is a frequent national conference speaker. With a profound passion for coaching and inspiring others to lead quietly, she is committed to a path of lifelong learning and teaching.

M.J. has a master's degree in organizational communication from The Ohio State University and a bachelor's degree in public relations from Ohio University. She is Accredited in Public Relations and was inducted into the Public Relations Society of America's College of Fellows in 2016. Before ILS, M.J. ran M.J. Clark Communications, a public relations, marketing and advertising consultancy, for 11 years and taught public relations classes as a visiting professor at Ohio University. Contact M.J. at mj@integratedleader.com and find her books and other materials at www.mjclarkbooks.com.

What Did You Think of
Shut Up and Manage?

Thank you so much for reading my book! I know the world is filled with great books about management, and I'm so humbled that you have chosen to add mine to your collection.

If you think this book adds value to your management practice, please **share your thoughts on social media, buy this book for your team, or share this book with a friend**.

If you enjoyed the book and found it beneficial, I'd also like to hear from you about what resonated most. If you could take some time to **post an honest review on Amazon and/or Goodreads**, I would be sincerely appreciative. I will use your feedback to make any future books better.

If you want to explore working with me as a consultant to your leadership team, as your executive coach, as a speaker for your event, or as your workplace trainer, please **contact me at http://www.linkedin.com/in/mjclark22, email me at mj@integratedleader.com, or visit www.mjclarkbooks.com.**

I look forward to connecting with you!

Sincerely,
M.J. Clark, M.A., APR, Fellow PRSA

NOTES

NOTES

www.ingramcontent.com/pod-product-compliance
Lightning Source LLC
Chambersburg PA
CBHW051737020426
42333CB00014B/1356